Guishsche, Where It All Began

RIGHT PLACE, RIGHT TIME

The Journey of a Pueblo of Laguna Native

Robert C. Carr
Guwatimu

Revised Edition

All About Indians Press, LLC
Albuquerque

RIGHT PLACE, RIGHT TIME
The Journey of a Pueblo of Laguna Native

Copyright© 2013 by Robert C. Carr (Guwatimu)

Library of Congress Control Number: 2013919279

Revised Edition, 2014
ISBN: 978-0-9860615-4-7

Published by All About Indians Press, LLC
aaipress@yahoo.com

All rights reserved. No part of this publication may be reproduced in any form, or by any means, without written prior permission of the author.

Front Cover design by Stephanie Carr, 2013
Ruins of Family Sheep Camp at Skro kana

Photos as noted by Rhiannon Carr, 2013

Book design by Patricia Merriman Carr

For

My parents, Pedro and Edith Pacheco Carr
The best teachers of what is to be valued in life

The people of Guishsche
Whose daily lives exemplified our values

Ganado Mission faculty and staff
Who acknowledged and nurtured my potential

The Roy and Jo Garten family
Whose home provided me refuge

My wife, Patricia Merriman Carr
Whose company brought meaning to my journey

Robert Charles Carr
Guwatimu

Table of Contents

Introduction		1
1	My Family	5
	My Mother and Father	
	My Brothers and Sisters	
2	Journey Begins in Guishsche, 1940's	19
	My Village of Guishsche	
	Guishsche-mahtra (People of)	
3	Growing up in Guishsche, 1940 – 1952	31
	Childhood Responsibilities	
	Fun Growing Up	
	Foods of My Childhood	
4	My Early Years as a Sheep Herder	59
	Draught Takes Family to Oklahoma	
	Returning to School	
5	Education of my Early Relatives	79
6	My Education Begins, 1945–1952	83
	Paguate Day School	
	Break up of Family	
7	Boarding School Years, 1952 – 1958	87
	Brief Stop en Route to Ganado	
	Ganado Mission	
	Happy to Get to Ganado	
	A "Work-Study" School	
	Life in the Dorm	
	Never a Dull Moment	
	Extra-Curricular Activities	
	Interpersonal Relationships	

      Athletics
      I Actually Attended Classes
      Westminster Fellowship
      Planning for College, Spring, 1958
      Leaving Ganado
      Home Together, a Rarity for Family

8 Summer, 1958   131

9 College Years, Part I, 1958 – 1960   135
      College of Emporia, Kansas
      Summer at Home, 1959
      Guishsche Undergoing Major Changes
      Sophomore Year, 1959 - 1960
      Decision to Transfer
      Last Summer Living at Home, 1960

10 College Years Part II, 1960 -1962   157
      New City and School
      The University of Tulsa Experience
      Living and Working in Tulsa
      Home Away from Home
      Graduation in Sight, Spring, 1962

11 Summer of Transition, 1962   171

12 Introduction to Social Work, 1962   175
      My First Job
      On to More Schooling, 1963
      Return to Oklahoma, Summer, 1964
      Tama, Iowa, Summer, 1965
      Back to Graduate School, 1965

13 Social Work – The Right Choice   185
      Move to Iowa City, Iowa
      The University of Iowa Hospitals
      Move to Minneapolis, Minnesota
      Exciting Years at Indian Center

14 Bureau of Indian Affairs, 1973 – 1999	203
Reflections on My Journey	215
Acknowledgements	217
Afterword	219
Sources	225

Note

I've used two tribally published dictionaries[1] for some of the Laguna words and phrases used in my story. Those taken directly from the dictionaries are noted with an * asterisk the first time they are used. I've spelled the others phonetically, including the names of my family members. Hopefully I've done justice to the pronunciations of the Laguna words and names with my phonetic spelling.

My description of the customs and the everyday life of the people of my village would be similar to those of the five other Pueblo of Laguna villages. However, my entire first twelve years of life were spent in my village of Guishsche and at our family sheep camps during a period when there was limited transportation. Therefore, I've described only what I observed and took part in while growing up in my village.

Laguna is short for Laguna Pueblo, the name of my tribe. Laguna is also the name of one of the villages, K'awaika*, where the tribal headquarters are located. I've referred to our language as Laguna, rather than Keresan, which is the spoken dialect of my tribe.

The suffix, "mahtra", phonetically spelled, means "people of". For example, K'waigame*-mahtra, refers to the people of the village of Laguna, as well as the tribe. My village of Guishsche and my reservation will always be home to me, so when I speak of home, I could be referring to my family home, my village, or my reservation.

While we are still referred to as Indians today, I imagine depending on the locale, the term Native American started being used in describing us beginning in about the 1970's. I've used both terms throughout the story.

The few vital statistics I used came from family records, Bureau of Indian Affair documents, and a Family Tree prepared by my late sister, Edna Carr Smith.

I've repeated some of the stories I told in "Robert Carr", HOME, *The Blueprints of Our Lives,* edited by the former Senator, John Edwards. See Sources.

K'awaika
Village of Laguna
Photo Taken by Rhiannon Carr

View of Guishsche
Photo Taken by Rhiannon Carr

Introduction

Right Place, Right Time. The Journey of a Pueblo of Laguna Native is the story of my journey that began in the small village of Guishsche on the Pueblo of Laguna Indian Reservation in New Mexico. I am a Kawaigamah, Guishsche mahsta. I am a member of the Pueblo of Laguna Indian tribe from Guishsche.

This is the way we generally introduce and identify ourselves. My Laguna name is Guwatimu. It was only after I began elementary school that my English name began to be used by the teachers. Outside of school though, I continued to go by my Laguna name.

In 1940, I was born into a family that already consisted of six brothers and sisters to parents who had lived their entire lives within the confines of the reservation. My mother and father had 4th and 7th grade educations, and like some of the other people in our village, their livelihood was dependent on our family's herd of sheep and the produce they raised in their small irrigated fields. I grew up in this environment during what may have been the last decade of life as it had been lived by the people throughout its history.

In the early 1950's uranium was discovered on the outskirts of my village, and the Anaconda Company began the Jackpile Mine operations in 1952. These two events abruptly changed many aspects of the daily lives of the people because for the first time local employment became available.

At the age of twelve, like most of the other children my age, I left home to attend boarding school away from the reservation, thereafter returning home only during some of the summer months and Christmas holidays. Up to the age of fifteen I spent my summers herding sheep. Despite the short span of time I actually spent growing up in my village, my first twelve years were lived in a culture

Right Place, Right Time

that clearly defined the roles and responsibilities we had to one another, to the tribe, and to the environment.

The people had their native religious beliefs and practices, but I was not a part of it, as we were never encouraged by our parents. However, we spoke one common language that contained the vocabulary to perpetuate the common values and traditions of our tribe as most of us did not begin speaking English until we entered the local day school.

In addition to the impact of my tribal culture and the manner in which my parents raised me, there were other important influences that affected the direction my life eventually took. Two early influences were the Presbyterian Church and the educational experiences of my relatives on both sides of my family. These two influences led to the enrollment of all the Carr children in the Presbyterian Church's boarding school, Ganado Mission, located on the Navajo Reservation in northeastern Arizona, rather than being enrolled in a government boarding school. My experiences at this school spurred me on to what turned out to be a most dramatic journey. It led to places I had never heard of and experiences I did not even dream about as I trailed after a flock of sheep from early morning to practically sunset out in the hot desert sun. Even more remarkable were the appearances of people at critical junctures in my journey whose encouragement spurred me on to the next segment.

After receiving my graduate degree, two federal rulings were enacted, and another was reaffirmed by the U. S. Supreme Court. In the absence of these rulings, I would not have been able to experience all that I have. The places where I worked would have been difficult for me to enter as an Indian during the period in which my story takes place.

Added to all these events were some decisions I made without thinking of the possible consequences that turned out as if

Introduction

they had been well thought out. For me, it's been an extraordinary life, in view of the time and place where I was born and raised.

I have purposely stayed away from any discussion of my tribe's religious practices. However, I was able to see the beauty of our ceremonial and traditional practices. I also saw how the people put into practice their values through their everyday lives. It is these early experiences that the values of the Kawaigamahtra were rooted in me. What I learned from growing up in their midst helped me weather some of my difficult experiences.

What I experienced once I left home may have been no different from the experiences of other Indians of my generation. During the period in which my story takes place, most of us were products of Indian boarding schools, and there were very few of us going on to college at the time. There was always much uncertainty about whether we could succeed without the support systems we had at home and what we developed in boarding schools.

There was also a very real sense of isolation. This was especially so for those of us who went to schools where few, if any, Native Americans were enrolled. If we ended up far from the reservations, we could not get home often. The primary means of communication at that time was by mail. This made it extremely difficult to maintain close contact with our families.

Many aspects of my story were difficult to write as I was raised in a culture that emphasized the notion that one did not bring attention to oneself. Bragging was definitely frowned upon, and I'm hopeful my story will not be seen as such. However, I wrote *Right Place, Right Time* to illustrate through my experiences about what is possible. To go from sheepherding to professional training, then going on to administer organizations and programs, and traveling to faraway places are what happened to me. I'm hopeful my story illustrates the crucial roles families and communities play in preparing their children for their future endeavors.

Right Place, Right Time

My story tells about my struggles with isolation and problems of adjustment in college. The story is also about the people I met along the way who gave of themselves to help me to keep moving forward, despite some of the issues that confronted me. If it were not for these people, my story would be quite different. It is my further hope that my story will encourage young Native Americans to learn as much as they can about their tribal customs and traditions. This knowledge will serve as a part of their foundation from which to build for whatever journey they undertake, just as I have experienced.

Right Place, Right Time chronicles the impact of family, tribal culture, education, social policies of the country, and people I met. As you will see, I always happened to end up at the right place, at the right time.

Brothers and Sisters at a 4th of July Gathering

Chapter 1
My Family

My story is based almost entirely on memories, both mine and my siblings, as well as on stories I've heard told about my early relatives. I initially thought of researching the census reports that were taken after 1850 for information about my great grandparents. However, it immediately became obvious that I'd have to devote much more time researching this background information. I found that some of the birthdates, names, (their spelling varied between reports), conflicted with some of the information contained in documents in the possession of my family. Anyway, I determined that any information I might gain from this research would not add significantly to my story, which is about the influences my family and others had on me.

About the most interesting thing I found in my cursory review was that dad's official name may have been Fred, rather than Pedro as we had always known him. One of the census reports listed a child by this name as a member of his nuclear family that approximated his birth year.[2] I also learned that my mother's family surname was spelled Pochako, which is now spelled Pacheco. Laguna names, spelled phonetically, were also recorded in the census data.[3]

My family's surname, Carr, came about as a result of my paternal grandfather having attended the Indian Industrial School, the first government Indian boarding school that was opened, in Carlisle, Pennsylvania in 1879 and closed in 1918. Linda F. Witmer in her book, *The Indian Industrial School, Carlisle, Pennsylvania, 1879-1918*, describes an event and a program at the Industrial School that, I'm assuming, led to my grandfather's first and last names, Charlie Carr.[4] As far as I know, he left home for Carlisle with only his Laguna name, Tzinaa'teyea.

Right Place, Right Time

In her description of the event, she tells about how the new arrivals at the school were taken into a classroom containing a blackboard. Through an interpreter the new students were instructed to pick what were "marks" written on the board. These "marks" were names, and what they would pick would be their name from then on. The list, I'm assuming, must have consisted of given names, so I'm guessing that our surname came from a family with whom my grandfather either lived or worked for in the school's "Outing System" as a student. This program placed students with families for whom they worked and lived with during the summer time as they were not able to return home.

I will be writing mainly about my mother's side of the family. The Pueblo of Laguna is matriarchal in its social structure so I grew up within my mother's side of the family. My father moved into my mother's family home when they got married, and his responsibilities also shifted to her family. We, the Carr children, also assumed our mother's clan, Y'aak'a* Hanu*. Y'aak'a actually refers to a dried ear of corn, and hanu means people. Today, our clan is often referred to as the "Corn Clan". I prefer the use of Y'aak'a Hanu over Corn Clan.

Because of the tribe's societal structure, my early childhood was centered on my mother's family. This structure affected to some degree the side of the family I know more about. Too, the early deaths of my paternal grandparents also limited my knowledge about them, and I never heard my dad talk about them. He may have done so with my older brothers and sisters.

In the course of writing this story, I've been particularly impressed by the similarities in the traits associated with my early relatives and those of my parents. The more stories I heard about these early relatives, the more impressed I became of the influences they had on my parents. Mother and dad in turn imparted to us what they had been taught about what was to be valued in life.

Chapter 1 My Family

The actual length of time I lived with my family could be seen as limiting my story. However, it is because of this very fact I find my experiences, as well as those of my brothers and sisters, to be truly remarkable. This is the story I want to share, beginning with my immediate family.

My Mother and Father

Zawaduetsa.
Edith Pacheco Carr.

My mother was born July 29, 1905, according to the notes in her aunt's Bible. *"The Bureau of Indian Affairs Census Roll"*, dated July 1, 1980, gives her birth year as 1906. She was the third of four children born to Francisco and Marie Pacheco and was the only girl in the family.

She was around eight or nine years old when their father died in a horse/wagon accident. Her oldest brother, Robert, would have been about twelve years old at the time, and their youngest brother, Lawrence, would have been an infant. We know little about our grandfather because of his early death, and mother never talked much about him, other than telling my older sisters that her father "left them" at an early age. Their mother remarried rather quickly after the death of their father.

Right Place, Right Time

She told my older sisters that her two older brothers either did not want their mother to remarry right away or they didn't want her to marry my step grandfather. They told their mother they would "take care of her" even though her oldest brother, Robert, was not even a teenager at the time. Whether it was because of these remarriage issues or other factors, the relationship between the children and their stepfather never became very close.

In addition, their relationships were eventually affected by issues involving the ownership of livestock and property that my grandmother's family owned. I never did learn whether my step grandfather had any livestock of his own. I am under the impression that the relationship between the children and their stepfather remained unchanged; however, I don't recall my mother ever treating my step-grandfather in a disrespectful manner even though she may have had feelings similar to those of her brothers.

My mother and her siblings did have a most caring and loving grandfather whose name was Felipe Sarracino. He became, or was already, a stabilizing influence in what appeared to be an unhappy situation as a result of my grandmother's remarriage. I tend to think that he may have already been the family "patriarch" judging from the way my mother described him.

From the descriptions I've heard about him, he was a successful and generous individual. He owned a large herd of sheep. According to a government document,[5] he dipped 1424 ewes and lambs for scabies, a rather sizeable herd in 1920. He would also bring back ewes he didn't want bred for the villagers to butcher for their families.

He also farmed and freely shared what produce he raised in his fields. One of the crops he raised was wheat, and my mother told one of my sisters how she got so tired of eating wheat bread. Great grandfather Felipe also served as a Scout for the U. S. Cavalry. The

Chapter 1 My Family

Pueblo of Laguna had been allowed to form its own U. S. military company, U. S. Cavalry Company I, in 1882.[6]

My mother idolized her grandfather. She told of an incident where a relative was criticizing her grandfather involving an aspect of his behavior. According to our mother, she responded by telling the relative that her grandfather may be whatever this particular relative believed he was, but he was the one who "fed her family". Very early on her grandfather appeared to have been a central figure in her life, maybe even eclipsing the roles of both my grandfather and step-grandfather as head of the family.

Whether it was due to the unsettled familial relationships resulting from her mother's remarriage, our mother apparently assumed a major responsibility in the care of her brothers. However, caring for her siblings at such an early age seemed to have been an accepted practice during those times, so it may have been a natural assumption of responsibility that my mother took on. I do tend to think that this also resulted from the less than positive atmosphere that seemed to have engulfed the family at the time.

At a very early age my mother was beset with serious eye problems. One of my sisters thought that it might have been trachoma. As a result she spent a lot of her very early childhood in government hospitals, one as far away as Ft. Defiance, Arizona. There is some suspicion in my family that the early ways that doctors treated trachoma may have further damaged her eyesight. She was never determined to be legally blind, but she always had limited vision.

I never heard her use her poor eyesight as an excuse for anything. She later managed her Type II diabetes, for which she had to take insulin, well enough that she lived to be eighty nine years of age. Because of her poor eyesight she was dependent on dad and my older sisters to prepare her syringes and inject her insulin, but her health problems never stopped her from living a full life.

Right Place, Right Time

I'm assuming that her eye problems and her numerous stays in hospitals away from home kept her from going beyond the fourth grade. However, the obligation to help her mother with the raising of her brothers may have been another factor.

Even though she did not get very far in school, she learned to read and write, as well as to speak and understand English as a result of being "home-schooled" by her aunt Ayche. Ayche, her sister and two brothers were educated at the Indian Industrial School. Mother apparently learned how to read quite well as my sister, Kathryn, said mother really enjoyed reading, and she often told them about the stories she read.

As an example of how well our mother learned to write, she kept a two year diary for 1934 and 1935, although most of the entries were made in 1934. Inside the front cover of the diary was written, "Bought by Mr. Lewis Lente, 1934." Lewis is her step-brother, who would have been about fourteen years of age when he purchased the diary for his sister. Practically all the entries related to the family's everyday life. She noted the date of her grandfather's death at their sheep camp, Skro kana, on May 28, 1934, and his burial at Guishsche on May 29, 1934. She also entered an interesting event that took place on October 13, 1934. John Collier, who was the U. S. Commissioner of Indian Affairs, 1933-1945, held a meeting for "all the people" at K'awaika. Our dad stopped to attend the meeting on his way back to his sheep camp that day.

Chapter 1 My Family

What really impressed me in reading her diary were her grammar and her hand writing. For someone with her educational background she learned to write extremely well, in fact better than some of us who went way beyond the fourth grade.

Zeeubaadru. Pedro Carr.

Our father. Our dad never learned of his actual birthdate. As he told it, his birthdate was made up for him by a local trader. Our dad evidently knew the season of the year he was born, so the month was established for him by the trader. How factual all this is I don't really know. Somehow the date of July 5, 1902 was settled upon as that date appears on the tribal records and the *"Bureau of Indian Affairs' Certificate of Indian Blood"*. I wish I had learned about his other name, Fred, before he passed away to see if that was his real name and what he would have said about it. Knowing him, he would have just laughed about it.

In addition to my grandfather being educated at Carlisle, three of his brothers and my grandmother were also educated at this school. These three brothers left Carlisle with different surnames: Stokes, Hudson, and I believe, Francisco. My grandmother even came home with the surname of Carr as she and my grandfather evidently got married while students at Carlisle based on the name change found in the Industrial school's student roster.

One of these brothers, dad's uncle, Frank Hudson, played quarterback for the Carlisle football team from 1895-1899 and was noted for his drop-kicking skills. He was named first team quarterback by *Outing* magazine's 1898 College Football All-American team and again in 1899. He was also a Walter Camp selection as a 3rd Team All-American in 1899.[7] This particular uncle remained in the East after he left Carlisle and never returned home.

Dad was the third oldest of the four boys born to Charlie and Belle Carr. I only learned of his Laguna name after I began writing

Right Place, Right Time

this story. People had always addressed him as Baadru. My sister Kathryn told me that she too never knew his Laguna name until one time her playmates were calling him Zeeubaadru. She thought they were calling him names. She told mother what they were calling him, who then told her that was her father's Laguna name. What I always thought was his name was actually a shortened version of his full name. Not knowing his Laguna name was actually not that unusual as the traditional way of addressing people was according to our biological or clan relationships to them.

My dad only went as far as the 7th grade before he dropped out of the Albuquerque Indian School. The story is that he got into trouble at the school because he used his winter cap, kuchuchu, to handle a tool or whatever he was working with in his shop class. His instructor got angry with him and may have punished him for it. So he ran away from the school and walked all the way from Albuquerque to Guishsche or his family's sheep camp. The walk would have been between forty to fifty-five miles, depending on whether he returned to Guishsche or to his family's sheep camp.

Once he left the Indian School, he never returned to school. My brother-in-law, Francis, who worked at the uranium mine on the outskirts of Guishsche, met one of dad's former schoolmates at the Albuquerque Indian School, who was also working at the mine. After telling the man he was married at Guishsche, he asked Francis if he knew Pete Carr. Yes, Francis knew him, as he was his father-in-law. The man asked if his father-in-law still chewed tobacco. Evidently he was already chewing tobacco as a twelve year old, a habit he did not give up until much later in life. He always carried the tobacco he chewed in his shirt pocket. It came in a block form about the size of a deck of cards.

Our father practically spent his entire life taking care of sheep, first his parents' herd, then his own. From the time he ran

Chapter 1 My Family

away from school and returned home, he devoted the remainder of his life to raising and herding sheep.

N'aishdiya* (Dad) on Left in Front

He eventually became the owner of a very large herd. One of my brothers thought at one time his herd numbered about 1600 head in the 1940's. By the time I began herding sheep as a five, six year old, his herd had already been greatly reduced as a result of the government's efforts to control erosion by limiting the size of herds. Dad had a well-deserved reputation as being a very successful owner of sheep, just like my great grandfather, Felipe. His flock always seemed to be the healthiest and the best cared for.

According to my mother, my great grandfather, Felipe, had recognized my father's attributes in caring for sheep. He must have continued caring for his family's herd after he married my mother as her grandfather Felipe had to tell him that he needed to cut his responsibilities to his family as he now had responsibilities to my

Right Place, Right Time

mother's family. This was in keeping with the traditional practices of the tribe.

Our parents were married in the local Roman Catholic Church on July 4, 1926. I've wondered why they got married in the Catholic Church. While my paternal grandparents were Roman Catholic, my mother's family was staunch Protestants. I later learned the reason for the marriage taking place in the Catholic Church was so that the marriage could be recognized. My mother was not quite twenty-one, and dad was about twenty three years old when they married.

My Brothers and Sisters

The Carr family grew rapidly after my parents' marriage. The first child, Kathryn, was born in April, 1927. My paternal grandmother, Belle Carr, named each of us. The tribe's traditional naming ceremonial practices, according to *Laguna Genealogies,*[8] was that the paternal grandmother was the one who named the newborn after washing the newborn's head. Apparently Grandma Carr was carrying out her traditional role. Regretfully, none of us

Dad and Elgin

Chapter 1 My Family

learned about the extent of any ceremony that took place, other than being named. The ceremony continues to be practiced. All of our names hold some meaning. I regret that none of us bothered to learn what they were. Elgin was given the name of one of grandfather Carr's brothers. I've only heard my name, or a word similar to it, used in reference to something growing, like plants in a field or garden.

Our grandmother gave us these names. I hope the spelling comes fairly close to their pronunciations.

Koohsghawetsa	Kathryn
Konamai Tsa	Alice Ethel
Duwa Gdro Tsa	Edna Lupe
Zuwaya	Elgin Earl
Kuwashoo Tsa	Evelyn
Kuwamai Tsua	Daniel
Guwatimu	Robert Charles
Sretimai	Walter Jacob

Edna, Kathryn, Florence (cousin), Alice, Evelyn

Right Place, Right Time

Our youngest brother, Walter, was born in May 1942. We had one other brother who died in infancy, so there were actually nine children born to my parents. Seven of us were born at home. I had always thought I was born in the Albuquerque Indian Hospital. It wasn't until I reached adulthood and got a copy of my official birth certificate that I learned I was also born at home.

Me and Walter

My brother Elgin told me how my English name, Robert, originated. He and our cousin, Robert Pacheco, Junior, were playing outside when I was born. Supposedly, Robert, Junior declared that my English name should be Robert after his and his father's name. I'm proud of being named after them. I have my paternal grandfather's name, Charlie, as my middle name although I've substituted Charles for Charlie.

All of us spent the first ten to twelve years living at home. Thereafter we all left to attend the Ganado Mission boarding school. Elgin and Walter were the youngest when they left; both of them were about ten years of age. Seven of us graduated from this school, and Walter completed his senior year at a nearby public school. In 1939, the year before I was born, our oldest sister, Kathryn, had already left home for Ganado, and thereafter, about every other year a Carr sibling headed there. Walter and I were the last to leave home in 1952.

Chapter 1 My Family

Daniel and Friend

Right Place, Right Time

Guishsche
Village of Paguate
Photo Taken by Rhiannon Carr

Chapter 2
Journey Begins in Guishsche, 1940's

My Village of Guishsche

The Laguna name of my village means "hand it to me". The story goes that as the People were migrating southward they came to the south edge of what is now Guishsche. As the people were handing their belongings down to each other over the plateau's edge, they probably used the phrase, Wehnu Guishsche, meaning "hand it <u>down</u> to me", but the village's name became Guishsche, "hand it to me".

My village is also known as Paguate. In the 18th century a man named Antonio Paguat (spelling uncertain) was given a land grant where the village is currently situated, and it was later purchased by the Laguna Indians.[9] Guishsche is located eight miles directly north of K'awaika, village of Laguna, and Interstate 40. At the time the two villages were connected by a well-maintained dirt road that later got graveled. Eventually sections of this road got rerouted and paved, to accommodate the uranium mine located on the outskirts of my village.

My village and the village of Encinal are isolated from the other four Laguna villages which are strung out over approximately twelve miles along the old U. S. Route 66 and the current Interstate 40. Both of the villages are located about six to eight miles north of these other villages.

The oldest part of Guishsche sits on a bed of solid sandstone rock along the southern edge of the plateau. There the edge drops several feet, which is where its name originated. The houses located along this edge served as a good lookout for their enemies, who in the 1800's were mainly Navajos and Apaches who often raided them. In fact, prior to the settlement of Guishsche, a two story

Right Place, Right Time

structure was built to serve as a watch tower and shelter for the people who came over from K'awaika to farm and herd livestock in the surrounding area.[10]

Paguate Watch Tower, Circa 1925

Photo and Caption from Wikipedia "Paguate"
http://en.wikipedia.org/wiki/Paguate,_New_Mexico
November 2, 2013

A 1925 photograph by E. S. Curtis, titled *Paguate*, shows two-story apartment-like structures along the south edge of the village, including a corn field below. This was what the village looked like about the time my parents married in 1926. Today the houses, which are no longer multi-storied, look pretty much the same, and several of the houses shown in the picture are still occupied. The corn field shown in the photograph is no longer cultivated.

The houses in the oldest part of the village are built right next to each other around the plaza where ceremonial events are still performed. All the houses, with flat roofs, are built of sandstone, plastered on the outside with a mixture of mud and straw. As one goes outward from the plaza to the west, north, and northeast, the houses become more spread out, and the lots become larger.

Chapter 2 Journey Begins

For example, our family land plot north of the village center is large enough to accommodate my maternal grandmother's house and ours. The Presbyterian Church is located in our yard because my family donated the land on which it sits. In addition, a large portion of the yard was cultivated at one time. This field produced corn and other vegetables, as well as fruit trees, all of which were beginning to be lost during my youth.

The primary source of heat for practically all the houses in the village was the wood-burning kitchen stove, which only heated the kitchen. The dried cedar wood used for the kitchen stove was hauled by horse-drawn wagons from the distant mesas, and one of the primary chores we performed as children was chopping wood and carrying it into the house. The kitchen served as the primary living area throughout the year, and during the winter months, it was the only room that was heated in the house. All the other rooms required the use of multi layers of blankets and quilts for bedding during the winter months. Since the houses were built of stone and without any insulation on the interior walls, the rooms were always nice and cool during the summer, but cold during the winter months.

A Kerosene lamp was used for lighting. Since we only had one lamp, the kitchen was the only lit room in the house. The lamp chimney had to be washed often as it was blackened by the burned kerosene. My folks eventually got a lamp fueled by a non-kerosene fluid. This lamp used a mantle, which increased the illumination.

My younger brother, Walter, and I had to find out what would happen to the glass chimney if we spat on it. We found out real quickly when the glass chimney shattered. I'm sure punishment followed this experiment. We had to revert to the use of the kerosene lamp again until another chimney and a new mantle could be purchased.

We slept on the floor. Eventually my bed consisted of two long wooden benches placed side by side with my mother's home

Right Place, Right Time

made wool stuffed mattress on it. My mother made the mattresses, and what I remember of them was how a "mold" was created in the shape of our bodies, personalizing our beds. At the sheep camp we either slept on the floor or outside in the open. We used mainly pelts for our bedding. About the first time I began sleeping on a store-bought bed was at boarding school. I did sleep on the couch when I stayed at my sister Edna's apartment in Albuquerque.

The water for household use came from one of the four water hydrants that served the different parts of the village. At three of these sites there were concrete watering troughs for the horses. One of our daily chores as children was going after water from one of the water hydrants. Luckily one of them was located only a short distance from the house. We kept the drinking water in a large dampened burlap-covered clay pot which gave the water a nice cool earth-flavored taste. We used a dried gourd that was cut in half as a dipper, and a metal basin sat on a wooden wash stand for washing.

The water source for our consumption was piped from a spring located just west of the village. This spring is referred to as Gahweashtaya. The name refers to the cold temperature of the water. The water source for irrigation is a dam located farther west, from which the water is delivered to the fields by a network of irrigation ditches.

Mother washed our clothes in the creek that ran below the south edge of the village. Kathryn remembers having to carry the clothes down and back in a wheelbarrow. I played in the water as she washed the clothes. At times other women went with her to wash theirs. In the late 1940's the local government day school began allowing the people to wash their clothes in the school's laundry room. The laundry room had tubs and running water which of course beat having to go down to the river to wash. About the same time, the school also began allowing the people to use the

Chapter 2 Journey Begins

showers in the student bathrooms. We took advantage of it since we lived right next door.

Before then my Saturday bath was in a round galvanized tub. The more "affluent" people owned the long galvanized ones, and we eventually got one. The bathwater was heated on the wood-burning kitchen stove, and mother scrubbed us with a smooth stone to remove the munaane, filth, off of us. Our skins must have looked pretty raw after these scrubbings.

The dried root of one particular yucca plant was used as a shampoo. The roots were first soaked in water to soften them. After they softened, the roots were then swished back and forth in water to produce the suds. The sudsy water was used to wash our hair. The adults would marvel at how clean and shiny my hair looked afterward as I spent what seemed like forever madly scratching my head. The soap really made our heads itch, and I hated having my hair washed. Either shampoo was not sold in the local store then, or my mother just preferred the original yucca-root-based shampoo.

There was only one telephone in the village that may have been tribally supported for use in emergencies. According to our former Governor, Roland Johnson, the first village telephone was located in his grandparents' home, and he and one of his cousins delivered the messages.

The one I was familiar with was located in another resident's home. I can't recall what the telephone looked like, but it certainly wasn't the kind you dialed; nor did it come with a Call Waiting or a Caller ID system. The lady in whose home the telephone was located acted as the "Operator" and was responsible for delivering the messages to the individuals who were called. I once accompanied my mother to respond to a call, and I remember how loudly she had to speak to be heard.

Since this was decades before email, web sites, etc., we had a Town Crier, Kukaadze eta. He would walk through the village and

Right Place, Right Time

at strategic locations he would make his announcements in Laguna in a loud and clear voice that could be heard and understood. He would announce such things as meetings, community work, and other information to the people.

All of the roads were unpaved. When it rained or snowed, they became extremely muddy, with the exception of the road between K'awaika and Guishsche, which was graveled and well maintained. We used to get much more snow than we do today. One of our chores immediately after a snowfall was to clear paths to important sites in the yard. The paths to the wood pile, the outdoor toilet, the chicken coop, the pig pen, and a path between my grandmother's house and ours were prioritized. Snow also had to be shoveled off the roof tops immediately to prevent leaks.

Much of the modernization of the homes began after the people became employed at the uranium mine and after I had left home. Many of the people now had the resources to install indoor plumbing, including bathrooms, wiring for electricity, and linoleum to cover the dirt floors. Propane came into use for heating and cooking. Gone are the outdoor toilets; the pig pen; the chicken coop; the wood pile; the fruit trees, and the cornfield and vegetable gardens within the confines of what remains the Carr family property. All this land had been previously owned by my maternal grandmother's family.

Daily Lives of the Guishsche-mahtra

As I became more aware of the people around me I saw how hard they worked day in and day out. The women were always occupied tending house, cooking, working in small vegetable gardens, baking bread indoors or in outdoor ovens, baa gaa dru tu, as well as carrying out other activities of daily living. Since there were no modern conveniences at the time such as gas stoves,

Chapter 2 Journey Begins

microwave ovens or washing machines, the women worked extremely hard caring for their families.

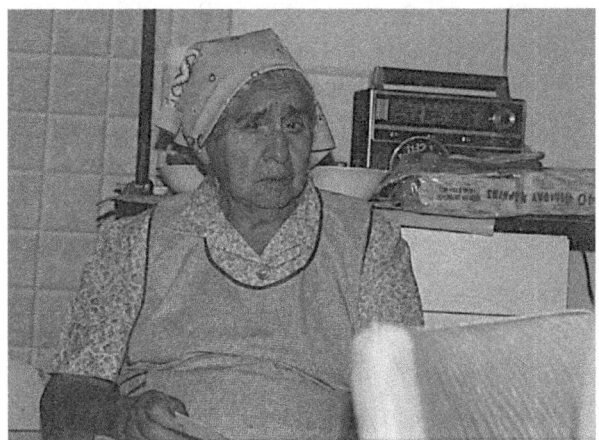

Sah Naya (My Mother)

The men worked just as hard, working out in their fields, hauling and chopping wood for the wood stoves, and carrying out community responsibilities. Those who were not around were tending to their sheep away from the village, like my father and grandfather. I don't recall seeing adults just sitting around unoccupied. There were some, of course, and they were referred to as tdu srah, lazy. As children we were not allowed to just lie around the house not doing anything; nor were we allowed to sleep late in the mornings. Sah mudi, tro epiti, my son, get up, snapped me out of my sound sleep each morning.

Except for the few people who were employed by the day school and the store, I was not aware of other paid employment locally until the uranium mining began. However, it is my impression that practically all the families possessed the basic resources to meet their needs. Mother occasionally remarked about some families being in need. While some aspects of child neglect or abuse may have existed then, I don't recall the subject being talked about.

Right Place, Right Time

The people did take time out from their daily tasks for various other activities, such as deer hunting by the men, piñon picking, "grab days", fiestas, and other celebrations and ceremonies. "Grab Days" and fiestas, in particular, were days of relaxation, laughter, storytelling, visiting, and eating. Even though we were tired by the end of the day, it was fun talking about and listening to all the funny events that occurred that day. People living away from the reservation returned to participate in the events. If there were dances, most of the day was spent at the plaza. My mother and grandmother spent their day preparing and serving meals to family and guests, taking an occasional break to go watch the dances.

One of my fondest memories of my childhood was hearing the jingling of bells as the dancers came out to dance early in the morning before the sun came up. The sound carried throughout the village, and as soon as we heard them, we went up to the plaza to watch the dances. Not much has ever matched the beauty of the setting and what I saw.

Up to this time all of us spoke primarily in Laguna, which helped us as children to understand what the roles and expectations were of us. By this time we had both Laguna and "English" names, although we were rarely addressed by our given names. As previously mentioned, we addressed one another using biological or clan relationships, i.e., brother, mother, uncle, etc. The relationship is preceded by the possessive pronoun, my, or Sah, in Laguna, then the given name.

For example, referring to my brother, Daniel, I would say, Sah dumu, Kuwamai, a shortened version of his Laguna name. If I did not know what my relationship was to an individual, I used the appropriate noun relating to the age of the individual being addressed. For example, I would refer to an elderly man as Sah nana, my grandfather, and then his given name. The word, Sah, emphasizes the importance of the relationship.

Chapter 2 Journey Begins

We were also taught very early on to show respect for all people. These lessons began with how mom and dad addressed us as children. My parents and my paternal uncles called me Sah mude, my son, and my sisters were referred to as Sah magou, my daughter. My maternal uncles called me Aanawe*, word for nephew, or uncle, and they referred to my sisters as Naya*, mother.

Generally the only time my first name was used was if others were present or I was in trouble. Then my given name, Guwatimu, was used. Today I address my two granddaughters by the Laguna word for granddaughter, Baaba'a*. If both are present and I want to address one of them specifically, I would say Baaba'a, Stephanie or Baaba'a, Rhiannon.

Another important lesson that related to ways of showing respect for others was to always acknowledge the presence of other people, particularly the elders. For example I pass by an older adult sitting outdoors; rather than just passing by without saying anything, I would say, Ayss tra ah, Na Na, acknowledging him sitting there and addressing him as grandfather. The person may respond, Ha ah, Na Na, Yes, grandson. That may be the extent of the exchange, or I could ask how he was.

This exchange addresses the importance of interpersonal relationships and respect for one another. As a young girl, my sister, Kathryn often saw this one elderly lady walking on the road that went by our house. This lady would sit and rest by a bridge over a nearby irrigation ditch, and Kathryn would run over to her and greet her, Dawa kde yah skra, Dya'au*, How are you, grandmother.

Expressions of gratefulness were used extensively. Men would say, Haawu*, thank you, after they finished eating. The women would say, Naidra*. Another expression we used when given water to drink is Pe-eh-cha, "May it rain!" The word, Dawaaeh, Thank you, is an expression of appreciation. It is also used to express gratefulness for a positive happening.

Right Place, Right Time

Many of these wonderful expressions of appreciation are still used, but may no longer be a regular part of the younger generation's language. There is one phrase that is expressed when parting, consoling or giving encouragement to a man faced with a difficult task that has remained particularly meaningful for me. That phrase is Hah tru tsa meh. Its literal translation is "Be a man, or act like a man". The context in which this expression is used is quite unlike how the word, machismo, is defined. I can't equate an English word or phrase that has more meaning for me than this Laguna expression.

Respect for the environment and what it provides for us is highly valued. Nothing was wasted. I saw this practiced by the care my parents took with their livestock. They also used practically every part of a butchered animal, such as sheep, pig, or deer. The same applied to how the fields and gardens were cared for, and what was produced. Water was only to be used for sustaining life.

Sharing what we had was especially valued, and this was practiced through the villagers' sharing of food, such as the deer dinners after the deer hunt and the "grab days". Sharing was a way of everyday life and was not restricted to only special occasions. What I and my brothers and sisters learned about sharing, came from our early relatives, such as great grandfather, Felipe, our parents, and the people of Guishsche.

Up to the time I entered the local day school, my first language was Laguna, and because we all spoke it, we had no difficulty communicating with each other. There was only one place where I heard English being translated into Laguna and that was in church where the entire service was translated. As more and more English began to be spoken, we entered a phase that increased the need to translate English to Laguna, and vice versa. It also affected the way we communicated with each other.

Chapter 2 Journey Begins

For example, directions and locations were always expressed according to the four points of the compass. In addition, they included topographical descriptions.   For instance, I meet an individual walking north as I am walking in the opposite direction. In my greeting, I would acknowledge the direction he is walking, with a description of the grade of the ground on which he is walking, such as whether it is sloping upward, downward, or level. We also didn't use the words, right and left, that we use today in giving directions. After I realized that many people today do not seem to know their directions, I've had to switch to using the words right and left in giving directions, rather than using the four points of the compass.

There are also many words, phrases, and expressions that are difficult to translate. They can also be interpreted in multiple ways. For example, my sister, Evelyn, and some of her female schoolmates were complaining about their elementary school teacher, using the phrase, Ah yah ah, an expression of annoyance or the English expression of "ouch.", Ko yho, old woman. One of their schoolmates heard them and reported to the teacher that the girls were saying, "Ouch old lady", completely changing what they were expressing, which was their annoyance with the teacher.

As we began using the English language more and more, Laguna words not used in our everyday communications become more difficult to remember. My sister, Kathryn, tells of how she and a co-worker needed to tell an elderly patient that he was going to get an injection. They couldn't remember the word for injection, so they told the patient he was going to get shot. He responded saying, Imii'i*, a male's expression of fear.

In another instance, a health worker didn't know how to tell the patient that he was near-sighted, so she told the patient he was stepping in place. The poor patient must have really been confused, as even I cannot understand the connection between nearsightedness and stepping in place.

29

Right Place, Right Time

This is a brief picture of the world I was born into and in which I lived the first twelve years of my life. All the expressions and practices that I have described are a part of who we are as K'awaigame-mahtra. There are certain aspects of my culture that I am not privy to, yet what I experienced was sufficient to nurture my growth and to form the foundation on which I was able to build throughout my journey. These practices have been hindered by the fast pace of our everyday lives; however, remnants of this early life still exist today.

Guishsche from the Southwest
Photo Taken by Rhiannon Carr

Chapter 3
Growing up in Guishsche, 1940 - 1952

Up until the age of twelve I lived at home and at the sheep camps with my family. My memory of events and the environment I grew up in only go back to when I was about the age of five. The earliest memories are of my family living with my maternal grandmother. While our own house was right next door to her's, we sometimes lived with her. It may have been due to her age and living alone, as our step-grandfather also spent a lot of time at the sheep camp.

I've always associated living with my grandmother with the ending of World War II. My family celebrated its ending by having a "picnic" outside my grandmother's house. A tarp was spread on the ground on which the food was set out, and on which we also sat. I doubt if we had today's typical picnic food, such as hamburgers or wieners, but I've always recalled this event as being quite special. The war's ending also ended the daily drones of large fleets of planes flying overhead which we were able to see and count.

Rationing of certain commodities for purchase is another activity I remember about World War II. Some of the ones I remember being rationed were coffee, flour, sugar, shoes, tires, and gasoline. I'm sure there were other items that I don't recall. I don't think we owned a vehicle at the time, so gasoline purchases may not have impacted us. "Ration books" were issued, I'm assuming to heads of households. These books contained stamps that the store keeper removed from the book as the rationed items were purchased.

I remember my parents talking about the rations as there were limits on what was allowed to be purchased. After getting home from the store, they would store some of their purchases in a

Right Place, Right Time

dirt cellar located beneath a small closet in the house. Whether it was one of the rationed items, I especially remember "butter" coming in a block form and my mother having to mix in an orange powder. I don't know if it was to give the "butter" color, or to add flavor.

Another event I associate with the ending of World War II was the return of a soldier's body for burial. I and some of the children gathered outside the Catholic Church to watch a hearse deliver the soldier's coffin. This was really a sad event. This was the first time I had seen a hearse, and even today seeing a hearse brings back memories associated with the solder's return home.

Until about the age of fifteen, my "summer home" was the sheep camp. After we started attending boarding school, I and my siblings were driven directly from school to the sheep camp at the end of the school year. I remember distinctly that I was still herding sheep after my freshman year. I had received a watch for my graduation, and I spent the days checking the time to see how many more hours were left before we could corral the sheep. This watch also helped me become quite adept at telling the times of the day by just looking at the location of the sun to the horizon, as well as my shadow. I knew it was noon, and time to eat, when my shadow became barely visible, or when it was about an hour before we could corral the sheep for the night. My overworked watch was no longer working by the end of the summer.

My summer living arrangements changed as I grew older. In my younger years my younger brother, Walter, and I would return home with mother after the lambing and shearing seasons were over, which would be sometimes in June. Later, I would pretty much spend the entire summer at the sheep camp, returning home just before the beginning of the school year. The summer after my freshmen year was about the last time I spent all, or part of the summer herding sheep, basically ending my sheep herding career.

Chapter 3 Growing up in Guishsche

My father was away from home a lot taking care of his herd. We did spend the spring and part of the summer months with him at the sheep camp. As a result, the two adults who provided me with the daily guidance during my early childhood were my maternal grandmother and my mother, simply because of their everyday presence in the home.

My mother, who was the only female child in her family, and my grandmother, had a very warm and loving relationship. I don't think I ever heard them argue or speak harshly to each other. Both of them were especially kind and generous. Whoever came and knocked at the door was told, Ubu, come in, aaisuna chuguya, sit down, even if they did not know the person. The visitors were always offered something to eat or drink, even if it was just bread, or coffee, or water. If the family was in the midst of a meal, room was made for them at the table. This was a common gesture during that time. Kindness shown to a person was not determined by one's relationship with them. This practice was a common courtesy that was based on respect for one another.

When dad was able to get someone to care for his sheep, he spent time with us at home. He must have been home enough as he was able to plant and raise corn. We had a small vegetable garden behind the old village graveyard (Shoomu gahtrutu, house/home of the deceased) that I remember my parents tending. We had two or more larger fields that were cultivated, one being right in our yard and the others away from the village. Mother did have to take over the work in the small vegetable garden when dad returned to his sheep camp, and of course I and my siblings were part of this workforce.

My parents had a very warm and loving relationship, and they laughed a lot. They got teased a lot too, especially by our brother-in-law, Francis. During one State Fair week Francis asked my mother if she was interested in attending the Fair. My mother

Right Place, Right Time

immediately said yes, thinking he was going to offer to take her. Francis told her he was just curious. He probably took her anyway.

They helped one another and supported each other with practically everything, such as the work, decisions, and sharing equally the responsibilities in raising us. Dad even helped mother with some of the household chores, including helping her wash and dry dishes. I don't think very many men did this in the 1940's, as this was long before the man's role with household responsibilities became an issue. He had no qualms about sharing these responsibilities, and our respect for mom and dad came from seeing how they treated and supported each other.

I did not realize it at the time that the roles they played as parents, individually and jointly, were particularly noteworthy in view of the cyclical changes of where we lived during the course of the year. Mother played the primary parental role when dad was at the sheep camp. If both were present, they shared these roles equally. However, mother was the primary disciplinarian.

I do remember an instance when my dad either threatened to use his belt on me, or he actually did. This must have been a rare incident as I remember quite vividly it taking place just outside the front door. However, I always felt safe and secure with either parent, never dreading that I would be staying with one or the other. My brothers and sisters felt likewise as both parents were very much in sync with each other about their expectations of us. An expression we often heard from them was Amuu'u*, Amu'u*, male and female expressions of endearment, Sah mude, or Sah magu, my son, my daughter.

Evelyn says she particularly admired our parents for never comparing any of us with each other. They treated each of us according to our individual needs and personalities as there was a range of both among us. Mom and dad emphasized and forever reminded us to love one another, Amu noma sah kudrus.

Chapter 3 Growing up in Guishsche

Mother was diagnosed with diabetes while she was in her forties. Other than having to take insulin, it never disabled her. Dad, who stood no more than five feet, five inches in stature, was physically strong and healthy. He never seemed to tire, even after a whole day of walking while tending his sheep or doing physical labor. He would even walk home from his sheep camp, a distance of about twenty miles.

One time a motorcyclist stopped and offered him a ride as he was hitch-hiking home on Route 66. With the wind blowing in his face, his nose began running badly. He was too scared to loosen his grip on the cyclist's waist to blow his nose. Having to walk someplace never prevented him from fulfilling what he saw as his responsibility. One time he served as tribal governor for one day, and he walked to K'awaika, a distance of eight miles, for a tribal council meeting and back home. Public officials did not have access to limousines at the time. By the way, he walked fast, and he was also a bit impatient. Poor mother was forever having to say, baa naa a, wait. The tone also changed as she was hurried.

I was too young to be observant of how other fathers treated their children, but I have very fond memories of dad and how he treated us. As children, he always held our hand as we walked with him.

I also remember very vividly him singing the Laguna version of the song, *Brother John*. Kumenachebai, Kumenachebai, Kdomuuh John ----. He would also sing for Walter and me as we performed the deer dance, adorned with antlers cut from card-board, and using sticks as deer legs. I did participate in one tribal dance as a youngster. This was the Dah laa wah eh, a dance we generally referred to as Follow the Leader. What I remembered of this one experience was receiving a handkerchief from my partner's mother, a very simple gift, yet the memory of the event has remained with me.

Right Place, Right Time

My family was fortunate in that all of us were pretty healthy. Mom used whatever suggestions the government nurse, who came to Guishsche periodically to conduct clinics, gave her about health care. One suggestion, which I hated, was having to take a teaspoon of cod liver oil before bedtime. My mother always gave us a piece of hard candy to take away the taste of this awful tasting oily substance.

Another medical practice that evidently prevailed at the time was the automatic removal of tonsils. I learned that all of us had been taken to the Albuquerque Indian Hospital to have the procedure done. Evelyn and Daniel were taken to the hospital at the same time for this procedure. I went with several of my day school classmates, and I was the only one who ended up having to remain hospitalized after they were discharged. I don't know why. The medical folks may have had difficulty finding what they were looking for.

Elgin told us of returning home on a school bus with other children from Laguna after having their tonsils removed and being discharged from the hospital. He said a boy from the village of Mesita was discharged even though it appeared that he had not fully recovered from the procedure. We laughed when one of us asked if the person in charge on the bus just wished the youngster to have "a good day" as he got off the bus in Mesita. This story may have said something about the state of our health care at the time.

Mom and dad had two sets of expectations that we did not have any choice about whether we wanted to comply complying with them. The first was church attendance. Dad did not begin attending until much later in his life. His non-attendance never created any doubts in my mind about his belief in a higher power. Whether his lack of participation had to do with his Catholic background, or his traditional beliefs, I don't know.

Chapter 3 Growing up in Guishsche

It was mother who was in charge of our religious upbringing. She had tremendous faith in God. The God she believed in was a loving God, and believing in him made all things possible. Ways of worshiping him may vary, but the differences were to be respected as she seemed to believe that there was no single "right way" to worship him.

She practiced what she believed, especially how to treat others as well as doing for others. She was very sensitive to how people were treated, so how my mother lived her life was a testament to this deep and abiding faith. During this time we did not hear much about the discrimination against Blacks. When we did, she always used the phrase, Imi-i, amu'u, female expressions of fear and compassion

We did not say Grace before meals, and I don't think my mother even read the Bible at home. Her teachings were more often than not, expressing thanks and giving credit to God for whatever we had, whether it was for good health, rain, crops, etc. Dawaeh stra n'aishdiyasha, Yuusi. Thank you our father, God, was one of her common expressions. Sharing what we had with others was emphasized, including time devoted to helping others.

She always reminded us that "our father" would replenish what we gave others. As I grew older, I gained a greater appreciation of the depth of her faith. I especially admire, particularly in today's world, the fact that I never heard her use how she believed as a weapon against anyone, or any group. Her beliefs were very simple and basic, and it's had a great deal of influence on all of us.

Mother also believed Sundays were to be a day of rest so dad did not get much sympathy from her when he went after firewood and hurt his back chopping and loading the wood one Sunday. Evelyn said Sundays were the only days she did not have to look after Walter and me. Sunday sheep herding was an exception, and how I often wished this was a forbidden Sunday activity.

Right Place, Right Time

We may not have had Sunday school, as my earliest memories are mainly of having to sit through church services for what seemed like hours listening to the translation from English to Laguna. Very few people spoke or understood English at the time, and my maternal grandmother's brother, John Sarracino, did the interpreting for the minister. I do remember attending at least one summer Vacation Bible School because of the fun activities, especially after a summer of herding sheep. What stands out though was the Kool-Aid that was served, the refreshment of those days.

Our Christmases were connected to the church. We never had a Christmas tree until much later. There was always one in the church where we generally celebrated Christmases. Gifts were handed out after the Christmas services, and they always included a small brown paper bag containing hard candy, an orange, an apple, and assorted nuts. My brother, Walter, and I did accidently find out where mother hid the children's gifts that were going to be handed out after the church service. We found them under one of the beds at home.

Another stringent requirement which we did not dare violate as children was school attendance. Elgin was evidently the only one who was brave enough to challenge it. He is known as one who continually ran away from school, and it was always to the sheep camp that he headed. The sheep camps that he ran to were located ten to twenty-five miles away. Each time he ran away my parents, or someone else, went to pick him up to get him back into school.

Elgin told me that one time two of our uncles were bringing him home from the sheep camp for the beginning of the school year. They stopped to open a gate, and Elgin jumped out of the truck and ran off and must have returned to their camp. He laughingly told of outrunning the uncles as they tried to chase after him.

Since the day school was adjacent to our yard, I always figured that it would be pretty difficult to get lost, but Elgin managed

Chapter 3 Growing up in Guishsche

it. Elgin's enrollment at Ganado as a 4th grader was no doubt the result of his running away from school. The rest of us must have liked going to school, or we were too scared to challenge our parents. Anyway, if I ran away from home I don't think my destination would have been the sheep camp.

Both of my parents spoke English when they had to. My mother had the habit of acknowledging what was said with, "Oh yes". One time I went to the store with some friends who were more fluent in English than I was. The store keeper was showing us something and explaining it to us. I must have used my mother's expression "Oh yes" too many times as my friend got upset and told me to "quit saying that!".

Many years later while I was working in Minneapolis, there was a community organization named Twin Cities Opportunity Industrialization Center. During my orientation there I caught myself saying, "Oh, I see", suddenly realizing that I was repeating what sounded like the last three letters of the organization's acronym, TCOIC. Reminded me of my mother's, "Oh yes".

When we expressed envy of other children's clothes, mother always reminded us that as long as ours were clean that we should not be ashamed, nor be envious of what other children wore.

I must have been overly sensitive about what my clothes looked like. I had a pair of trousers that I thought were too baggy, and I was embarrassed to wear them. One time I took my mother's needle and a spool of thread and climbed our favorite apricot tree and sat in the tree and tried to sew the legs to reduce their bagginess. I must have had to take my pants off to do this. When I got through sewing, they looked worse than before, so I unstitched my work, put my trousers back on and returned the thread and needle.

I am still reminded today that as a child I always buttoned my shirt all the way to the collar. When my sisters tried to make me

Right Place, Right Time

leave the top one unbuttoned, I resisted it. Dad always had his shirts buttoned to the neck, so that's where I must have learned the proper way to wear a shirt.

Childhood Responsibilities

A lot of responsibilities were placed on us at a very early age. As soon as we were old enough we had chores to perform such as going after water, chopping wood for the stove, carrying firewood from the wood pile into the house, feeding the animals and chickens that were raised at home, hoeing in the garden, and generally helping our parents and grandparents with their daily chores. The older girls babysat their younger siblings and helped with the household chores.

Most of the chores we performed no longer exist today, except probably for those growing up in rural areas. So in many ways, I grew up during a period when many more responsibilities were placed on children at an early age. Harvest time was a particularly busy time for the entire family. The children were a big part of the workforce. We were expected to help our parents, and they also expected us to help other people with their harvesting.

There are three events I remember very clearly as being hard work, but also a lot of fun. One was helping to harvest wheat with a sickle. We once helped to harvest an entire field. By today's standards, the fields were small, but having to harvest wheat with a sickle made them look awfully big. At noon we were fed a big meal at the home of whoever we were helping, and then we returned to the field to finish the work. The work was tiring because you had to bend over to cut the wheat plant at its base in order to preserve the entire plant. It was also hot under the sun.

The field we harvested was located between the village proper and China Town, a cluster of homes located about half a mile west of the village. Apparently there are several versions of how the

Chapter 3 Growing up in Guishsche

name came about. According to one story I heard, the individual who originated the name thought this cluster of houses looked like a picture she had seen of "China Town." The name stuck as this locale has always gone by this name.

This field was also located in the vicinity of Gahweashtaya. Many of the larger grain fields were located in this wide valley as this was the most fertile area. Coming from K'awaika this area stands out when seen from the mesa because of the greenness of the fields.

After the wheat was cut, we hauled it by wagon to a specially prepared circular corral below the southeast edge of the village. After the wheat was spread out on the hardened surface inside the small corral, several horses were put in the corral and made to run in circles to thrash the wheat. Once the wheat was completely thrashed, the horses were removed, and the women entered the corral with large woven baskets into which the wheat and the chaff were placed. The women then tossed the content up in the air so the breeze could separate the wheat from the chaff, leaving the wheat in the baskets. The cleaned wheat was then placed in sacks. The straw was saved and used for mixing with mud for plastering houses.

During all this work, there was a lot of joking, storytelling, and laughter among the people. During this time no one was paid; nor was payment expected. A meal was generally the only "payment" received. These types of work were announced through word of mouth, and people generally showed up to help without being asked.

Another fun activity which stands out in my memory was the harvesting of watermelon and cantaloupes. My closest childhood friend, Phillip, and I would help his grandfather pick and haul his melons from the field that was located away from the village to the family home at the end of the growing season.

Right Place, Right Time

We were no more than ten years of age and weighed only around one hundred pounds each, and we were already harnessing our grandfathers' teams of horses without any help. His grandfather grew a lot of melons, and we had to make several round trips to haul all of them. Phillip's grandfather was really kind, and he always treated us so well.

The harvesting and the roasting of the fresh corn in the outdoor, domed oven, Baa gaa tru tu, was another big harvest event. After the fresh corn was picked and hauled to the house, our parents would prepare the outdoor oven by filling it up with dried cedar wood and burning it until it was hot enough. In the early evening the ashes were cleaned out, and the oven was filled with the green ears of corn. They then plastered all the openings, and the green corn was left in the oven over night for roasting.

This was an exciting event, especially for the children. We even got up early the next morning without being told to get out of bed for the opening up of the oven. As dad opened it up, a waft of the delicious smell of roasted corn came out. Everyone would take a still warm ear of corn whose husk had turned from a green to a tan color, pull back the husk and begin eating the kernels off the cob. Not only did we eat the kernels of corn, but the children also chewed on the still-moist sweet-tasting husks and sucked on the corn cobs.

Chapter 3 Growing up in Guishsche

The roasted ears of corn were tied together in twos and hung out to dry from a wire stretched along the eaves of the house. The corn was later used for food; some of it was ground and made into flour. Husks were saved to wrap tamales in and for other uses, such as lining for the bucket in which the Easter pudding was baked.

The corn remaining on the stalks out in the field was harvested later in the season. This corn was hauled to the house and piled outside. My mother and whoever else was helping her, sat by the pile of corn, removing the kernels by rubbing two ears of corn against each other. Most of it was used for our dietary consumption, and I'm sure that some of it was for livestock feed.

Our parents didn't know that the boys also used pieces of the dried cornstalk for smoking. We forced a strong piece of wire through the core, lit one end and smoked it. Boy, the smoke stung our tongues, so generally a few puffs were all we could handle in one smoking session, usually behind the barn.

There were other activities that went on involving the male children and adult men. One of these activities was the rabbit hunt. The men and young boys would hunt for rabbits, using sticks rather than firearms. I learned that these hunts were announced at dawn by the War Chief as they were not recreational in nature. They served other purposes for the people, in addition to the consumption of the meat.

Before we went off to boarding school, dad acquired horses for Daniel, Walter, and me. Mine was a pinto. We didn't keep these horses very long, except for Daniel's horse, Blaze. I'm assuming the others were let go because of the amount of care they required. Dad did own a mule whose name was Nancy.

Once when I was still quite young my father asked me to take Blaze to our sheep camp at Yagach'a,* located approximately twenty miles from Guishsche. I wasn't afraid of getting lost as I was already familiar with this part of the reservation, and I had a good

Right Place, Right Time

idea of the route I was to take. My father still went over the landmarks with me.

In order to have plenty of time to get there, I left home early in the morning. Sitting in the saddle was tiring, so I alternated between riding Blaze and walking. I would occasionally stop to rest and to eat the lunch my mother fixed for me. I made it to the camp without getting lost or running into any problems. Boy, was I saddle sore by the time I got there! At the time nobody seemed to think anything of asking a youngster my age to ride a horse this distance by himself, and I remember this assignment as being pretty special.

Because we did not know anything different, as children we just accepted the fact that growing up involved more work than play. As far back as I can remember we were responsible for helping around the house. In fact, before we could go out and play we had to complete whatever chores we had been assigned.

Kathryn, in the paper she later wrote for one of her classes at Ganado, talked about having to go right home after school, otherwise being punished if she didn't. The first thing we did after we got home from school was to change from our school clothes, as we generally wore them for a week at a time.

My sisters tell me that our mother was dependent on them to care for the younger siblings. Since Evelyn was the only girl left at home by the time I was five years old she was saddled with me and my younger brother's care. Her childhood girlfriend had similar responsibilities, so they had to take us wherever they went.

Only after adulthood did Evelyn confess to some "lapses of judgment", one of which was to allow Walter and me to slide down a steep sandstone slab at the south edge of the village which the older children used. We must have gotten scared or we got hurt, but she and her friend talked us into not telling on them. Other than confessing to this one incident, she and her friend must have been pretty responsible as Walter and I survived their care.

Chapter 3 Growing up in Guishsche

My siblings and I learned a great deal about responsibility while we were still quite young. Our parents always acknowledged our work. They were good at assigning us work we could perform. Because of this, we were able to experience success very early on, even if the assignments were not earth-shaking. Having to be accountable gave me an early start to understanding what it meant to be responsible. Despite all this, I have a lot of good memories about my early childhood.

Fun Growing Up

As I look back at this period of time, there really didn't seem to be that much free time available for what we now consider leisure time. I don't think our parents made conscious efforts to make sure that their children included a "healthy" type of activity in the course of the day. Their concept of healthy activity always seemed to be work related, and they never had any difficulty finding work to assign us. I'm making it sound as if all we did was work. We didn't.

There were no organized leisure time activities available in the village. The closest towns that offered recreational and entertainment activities were Albuquerque and Grants, approximately fifty-five and thirty-four miles away, respectively. Because we did not have electricity until just before I left for boarding school, we did not have television. We also had limited access to transportation, so we basically had to entertain ourselves. Since we never had access to the commercial entertainment that was available to kids living in the cities, we didn't know what we were missing.

Some of our recreational activities mimicked what went on in the village. We had fun enacting a celebration that was held for individuals named after Catholic Saints. There were at least four dates on which these took place during the summer months. To celebrate, the families who had members with such names gathered

Right Place, Right Time

on their roof tops and tossed food to the people who stood below to catch what was tossed. We referred to these celebrations as "Grab Days".

During my early childhood much of what was tossed was food that was produced by the families, such as fruit, vegetables, bread, and occasionally, mutton. After the uranium mining began, and local people became employed, they begin throwing primarily store-purchased products.

Before the food-tossing began, a family member, or whoever they asked, spoke to the crowd telling who the celebrant was, giving thanks for what they had, and hoping the crowd would appreciate what they were able to get. I always thought this speech was pretty special, especially the expressions of appreciation for what we were blessed with.

As soon as the speech was over, dippers of water were tossed on the crowd. In later years the tossing of water balloons became popular. The crowd would yell, Pe'echa!*, meaning "may it rain! Another yell was "Duwenu!" meaning "down this way", asking the throwers to throw the goods in their direction. Sometimes a whole bucket of water would be tossed, and if you were standing in the right place, you would leave drenching wet, which probably felt pretty good in the hot summer weather.

My parents told us that in earlier times there was a contest on these days in which men raced on horseback coming toward each other from opposite directions trying to grab a rooster that was partially buried in the ground. This very dangerous contest was eventually stopped after a contestant died in one of these events.

These "Grab Days" were a lot of fun for both children and adults as we went from house to house carrying what we had caught in flour sacks. Some of the men rode horses, and people from the nearby Spanish villages would attend these celebrations. In later years as people began owning automobiles, mainly pick-up trucks,

Chapter 3 Growing up in Guishsche

people would jump on the back of these trucks to go to the next house.

These Grab Days were just days of relaxation and visiting. When there was a lull in the throwing, people would sit in the shade of the houses talking and laughing. At the end of the day, we enjoyed eating the things we caught, and laughing about the day's efforts in trying to catch what was thrown. This particular celebration is a good example of how we shared what we had. These celebrations continue on a much smaller scale today.

Another fun activity took place during the fall deer hunting season. The men went deer hunting at locations of great distances. The hunters usually went in groups, generally consisting of relatives, and most of them traveled by wagon, going for days at a time. As the hunters returned, they would signal their return by lighting a fire at the top of Kuyachuku, which can be seen from the village looking southward toward K'awaika.

Photo Taken by Rhiannon Carr

Right Place, Right Time

About the time we thought the hunters would be returning, the young people would gather at the south edge of the village in the evenings to await this signal by the returning hunters. These gatherings were a lot of fun. We would build a small bonfire, and it got pretty exciting when we saw the signal. Even after we saw the fire, we'd still have to wait a bit longer for the hunters to reach the village due to the distance of about three miles.

Once we found out who the returning hunters were, we'd race to their houses where their families would display the deer. The head and the skin of the deer would be placed on the floor of one of the rooms in the house. There generally was a necklace and blanket adorning the deer. A small bowl of corn meal would be placed by the deer for the viewers to sprinkle on the deer head as a way of giving thanks for the sustenance it would provide the family.

The hunting season culminated in the traditional "deer dinner" sponsored by the hunter's family. A deer stew containing piñon nuts and seeds from locally grown crops was prepared, and guests were invited to the dinner. A certain female relative was given the honor of eating the various parts of the head; meat, eyes, brains, etc.

During the winter months mother would occasionally take us up to one particular female elder's home in the evenings to hear her tell us of the myths and legends of the people. These stories were referred to as Hama Ha, my interpretation as meaning "long ago". In fact the story telling would begin with this phrase. I can't recall any of these stories now. What I do remember was sitting spellbound on the floor by the storyteller's chair, either beside a warm stove or a fireplace, listening to her tell these fascinating stories of our people and their past. Elgin remembers the stories being told by a male story teller. Walking home afterward was cold, my younger brother, Walter was carried on my mother's back using her blanket as a sling to hold him.

Chapter 3 Growing up in Guishsche

As far as toys were concerned, most of them came as Christmas gifts from either the church, or from the "Minnehaha Club", a local women's group. The name must have been thought up by a government bureaucrat as the name has no connection to our tribe or the Southwest. Anyway, the toys were generally cars and trucks for the boys, and I do not recall toys like soldiers and guns, or other toys that are prevalent today.

During the summer we played in the shade of a large apricot tree located just north of my grandmother's house. My younger brother and I spent a lot of time climbing and sitting in its upper branches. This was the tree that I sat in sewing my baggy trousers.

We made some of our own toys. One favorite toy consisted of a metal rod and a metal ring. The rod, about three feet in length, had a rounded hook bent at an angle at one end. The other piece was a metal ring that was about an inch wide and no more than eight inches in diameter. The metal rod was used for rolling the ring along the ground. The process began by tossing the ring on the ground, like a bowler tossing the ball, then using the hook on the rod to push the ring forward in an up motion to keep it rolling.

Another home-made toy was made from a wooden clothespin. The clothespin was modified in such a way that the spring was used as a trigger for a match placed between the two wooden pieces. The burning match would shoot several feet. My brother Dan said that one time he and a friend fired a match into a haystack and started a fire. One of the village officials made sure this incident was reported to dad.

Sling shots were another favorite play item. We looked for wishbone shaped tree branches, and trimmed them to an almost perfectly shaped wishbone frame. We cut used inner tubes into strips, and a piece of leather for the shot holder. We hunted mainly birds using small pebbles for ammunition. During the fruit bearing season, we lay on our backs under the trees to wait for the birds.

Right Place, Right Time

We made another toy out of a thread spool. The spool ends would be notched. A rubber band was threaded through the spool hole, and small pieces of match sticks would be used at each end to hold the rubber band in place. The matchstick at one end was then used to wind the rubber band until it was fully taut. As the rubber band unwound, the spool would roll forward on the ground until the rubber band loosened.

Very few children owned store-bought recreational equipment, such as bicycles. A young boy whose family had returned home after living away owned a small child-size bicycle. It may have been one of the first bicycles to appear in the village as I was quite fascinated with it. We would go play with him hoping he would let us ride it, which he always did. This must have been where I learned to ride one.

It was not until after I went to boarding school that I bought a used bike. When I returned to school I stored it in our barn which was located away from the house. By the time I returned home for the summer, it was gone. One day as I was walking through the village, I saw a boy riding it. I can't recall whether he returned it voluntarily, or if I had to force him to give it back.

We spent a lot of time walking and playing on the nearby mesas. We also played in the two creeks that bordered the east and south sides of the village. The one on the east side was about a half mile away, while the other one was much closer. It was the latter that my mother washed our clothes in.

There was always water in these creeks in which we would play. There were places where the pools were deep enough to swim in. After it rained especially hard, we could hear the roar of the rushing water in the creek that was located on the east side. I would hear my parents describing the water rushing down the river, Maameh Wah Dwechumu.

Chapter 3 Growing up in Guishsche

In early spring we looked for and picked wild parsley, schamu, and onions east of the village. There was also a root that we dug up, peeled off the covering, and chewed. Another root we looked for and ate resembled bean sprouts.

Wild tea was another plant that was gathered and used. Boiled, it produced a dark orange-brown colored tea. I don't know how to describe the good flavor of the tea. Today, if one looks hard enough, wild parsley and onions can still be found, and the wild tea still seems to be plentiful.

There was one plant which seemed to grow at only one location west of the village. The plant consisted of rod like stems. This plant produced tiny amounts of sap at the joints of its stems which we removed and chewed. We called it "rainbow gum", k'ashdyaats'i-habashch'a*. When we chewed it, our saliva had a slight color to it. I don't know if that's why it was called by that name. The sap was sweet, and it was chewable, and it tasted good. This plant wasn't particularly plentiful, and it may not exist today.

Wild spinach was another plant that was gathered for food, which was pretty much done by adults. I associate the growth of this plant to be along the side of asphalt-covered roads, and where I saw the spinach growing was alongside of U. S. Route 66. At the time this was the only paved road that ran through the reservation. Later on there were some along the road between K'awaika to Guishsche after it got paved. The reason I associate the gathering activity with adults was because of the need for transportation to get to these sites.

Anyway, the entire plant was pulled, gathered, and placed in a pile in the shed that was attached to my grandmother's house. These plants were leafy and grew to about two feet in height. The plant also had a terrible smell. My mother and grandmother who removed the leaves didn't seem to be bothered by the stench of the wild spinach. The smell was so bad that I hated to go into the shed.

Right Place, Right Time

After it was cooked, there was no longer the strong odor, and mixed with other ingredients such as chili, it was really quite delicious.

Another occasional recreational activity was rounding up donkeys and riding them bareback. Most of this activity, however, took place at the sheep camp as donkeys were used for transporting our camping equipment as we moved the camp from site to site, dictated by the availability of grass for the sheep.

Even though the donkeys were short in stature, it hurt when they threw you. They were really good at throwing you off their back. Their favorite trick was to walk or run under trees where the branches would catch you across the upper body to get you off their back. They were also good at hiding from you. They would hide behind trees, and to find them, we had to track them. They were always hobbled, so they usually didn't wander very far, but they were still difficult to locate.

I did become an entrepreneur at an early age. I sold Cloverine, a salve which was quite popular during my time. My mother ordered the product for me. The order came in a tube containing about ten tins of the salve, which sold at about $.25 a tin. These orders included pictures of various subjects which the customer would select with each purchase of a tin of the salve.

This salve was used for soothing chapped hands and faces, a "jack of all trades" salve as it's currently advertised on the Internet. I tried selling another salve named Rosebud without much success, so I stayed with my best seller.

After all the salve was sold, the "salesman" became eligible to pick a reward from a catalog that accompanied the order. One time I had my eyes on a BB pistol for which I was eligible to order, and I couldn't wait for my mother to send in the receipts of my sales.

Chapter 3 Growing up in Guishsche

Guess what? I was made to order a box of school supplies instead. I was so disappointed.

This experience may have brought to a close my sales career. I also sold vegetable seeds for a spell, but there was nothing like selling Cloverine. Years later, I would still see the pictures on the walls of my former customers, reminding me of my rather successful career as a salesman. Kathryn told me she sold Rosebud, the product I wasn't successful at selling, and that one of my school mates also sold that same product in his youth. He must have sold his product in a different part of the village as I never ran into him.

I asked Kathryn how mother knew about such opportunities for us. She thought she might have seen the ads in magazines for selling various products. Even then, there were already a lot of ads, and I remember one in particular. It pictured a muscle-bound man, Charles Atlas, with the caption, "Are you tired of having sand kicked in your face?", or something to that effect. Mom evidently didn't think we had that problem as we didn't get involved with whatever product the ad advertised.

I find it quite unusual that we got this type of experience, particularly during this period of time in our rather isolated village. More surprising is that mother knew how to manage this activity.

What I have described about what I did growing up in the village changed rather drastically after the uranium mine opened. Local employment became available on a major scale for the first time, and the local economy changed from one where we were almost totally dependent on small-scale farming and sheep raising. Returning home, even after a couple of years away at boarding school, much of what we did as children was no longer being done.

Right Place, Right Time

Foods of My Childhood

Even though there was always a local store, we rarely had much money to buy candy and other sweets. We made do with homemade snacks which we either fixed, or were prepared for us. Since we did not have freezers or refrigerators, the only time we made homemade ice cream was in the winter time. Kathryn remembers having to go down to the creek below the village to get the ice to make the ice cream. Other than buying an ice cream cone at one of the fiestas, ice cream was a rare treat. Elgin said he got ice cream from the local store owner for helping him unload his supplies.

Jell-O was another item that was only prepared during the winter months. After mixing the ingredients, the container was placed outside the window at night in order for the mixture to gel.

During spring time as the pods on the cottonwood trees appeared, we would pick them off the tree. We took the cotton out of the pods and mixed it with the fat off of dried meat, which we chewed as gum. Another chewing gum was the sap from the piñon trees. I learned the hard way that one could only convert dried sap into a chewing gum.

One time at the sheep camp, I tried chewing the sap before it hardened. The sap stuck to my teeth, and it was impossible to remove it as it filled every space between my teeth. For days, the only thing I could taste was the piñon sap. This bad experience didn't stop me from trying it again. The next time I made sure the sap had hardened. We tried chewing the tar taken off the roofs of the government buildings when the sun softened it.

Another summer home-made snack was taking the fruit, idya*, off the cactus after they ripened. We pulled the fruit from the cactus plant using two sticks, grabbing the fruit as if one was using chop sticks to take a food item from a plate. We then used a small bush as a brush to remove the tiny hair like needles off the fruit. My

Chapter 3 Growing up in Guishsche

mother then dried them in the sun. After they dried, she ground the dried fruit on the grinding stone and mixed it with cornmeal to make haat'i*. This made a pinkish colored sweet tasting snack which we ate from a bowl with our fingers

One time my grandmother told me how good acorn tasted, and she promised me that the next time we went to the sheep camp I could pick some, and she would fix it for me to eat. From the way she talked about it I looked forward to eating it. The next time we went out to visit my grandfather at the sheep camp, I gathered fresh acorn that had fallen to the ground. I couldn't wait to get home so my grandmother could fix it for me.

I must have pestered her because she boiled them as soon as we got home. Finally, when it was ready it had turned into a mush-like substance, which she put in a bowl for me to eat. It not only looked awful, it tasted awful. I quickly found out that I didn't have the taste for boiled acorn.

At the top of my list for a good snack, other than store-purchased sweets, was a mixture of peanut butter and Karo Syrup. Mother must have thought it wasn't good for us as she didn't allow us to have it too often. I still recall the times we sat at the table eating this delicious snack. Sometimes my parents used Karo syrup in their oatmeal. Mother fixed pancakes for us on occasion, but it was grandmother's pancakes I remember. Another favorite snack was buttered saltine crackers. At the time it was margarine, rather than real butter.

Home grown agricultural products, mutton, pork, and eggs were the primary sources of food. My family did not own any cattle, and what milk we drank came from the goats during the spring. I don't think I drank dairy milk until I got to boarding school. I do remember drinking the canned evaporated milk on the sly and using it in my coffee at the sheep camp. My family always raised chickens, both for their eggs and for our consumption.

Right Place, Right Time

My family raised at least one or two pigs for butchering every year, and one of my chores was to feed them. There was always a slop bucket into which leftover food was dumped for them. I enjoyed listening to them chomp on watermelon rinds and corn.

One of the funny experiences we had in raising pigs was having to chase them when they escaped from their pen, which they were good at. One time in particular, we had to chase our pig through the village trying to catch it and return it to its pen. Dad didn't think it was much fun, while we thought it was hilarious, and so did the people who watched us trying to catch the pig.

We were finally able to get it back in the pen. As soon as we did, dad went back to the house. He went in through the front door and walked through the house to the back door where he usually sat on the door step to take off his shoes. By the time he went out the back door, the pig was already standing in front of him after escaping from the pen again! Boy was he mad. Later on, this incident became a story that we would laugh about. Even dad finally had to laugh about it.

Just like today, the local store had gimmicks to bring back its customers. One I remember participating in was getting a piece of dinnerware, like plates and saucers, every time I made a purchase. What we got depended on the amount of the purchase. I would beg my mother and grandmother to let me go to the store for them, and as I recall, I acquired quite a collection of dinner ware. I guess nobody saved them for me for my future use as I never saw them again once I left home.

One or two other family-owned stores opened up at different times, never surviving very long due to the small amount of business. One of the stores sold Joy Balls. Joy Balls were large jaw breakers, a round hard candy that was slightly smaller than a golf ball, attached to a rubber band. We must not have purchased enough of them for the store to stay in business very long.

Chapter 3 Growing up in Guishsche

Another store that opened up even sold sugar canes. The most money we ever had at any one time was a nickel or a dime to spend. Once Daniel tricked me into giving him my dime for his nickel by claiming the nickel was worth more, using the difference in the coin sizes for his claim.

I was fortunate to have grown up in Guishsche before the discovery of uranium. It allowed me to observe and to experience the richness of my culture. It emphasized and nurtured respect for one another, respect for nature, the value of sharing, and, most importantly, a community of people that looked after one another. The traditions, customs, and the one language we spoke governed our daily lives.

After the mining started and people became employed, it immediately impacted our daily lives and practices. The pace of life quickened, and the focus of our daily lives changed. If there was one event in the history of the tribe that severely impacted its traditional way of life, it was the discovery of uranium. I believe my orientation would have been quite different had I had lived in Guishsche after the mining began. So my history of being at the right place, at the right time really began in Guishsche.

Right Place, Right Time

Yagach'a

Chapter 4
My Early Years as a Sheep Herder

After my wife and I became grandparents, our two granddaughters were participating in their school's annual Christmas play in which one of them played the role of a shepherd. Her grandmother told her that her grandfather was a shepherd at one time. Her eyes widened, maybe thinking that I was that ancient and had lived during the Biblical times. I must point out that we were called "sheep herders," not "shepherds," and I was one during the summer months from the time I entered the local elementary school until I turned fifteen after my freshman year in high school.

During that period, springtime meant both the end of the school year and the beginning of herding sheep for at least part of the summer. By evening of the last day of school, we were already at the sheep camp. By the following day we were herding the flock we were assigned.

Springtime was an extremely busy time for the sheep growers as it was the lambing and shearing season. To accommodate the sheep growers the local day school ended its school year sometime in April. Mother always left for the sheep camp before school let out in order to help dad. My parents would arrange with one of the relatives to care for us temporarily until school let out, which often times was only for a week or two.

I never looked forward to these temporary stays with the relatives, despite their good care. It was the difference in their lifestyles and their expectations which I didn't look forward to each spring. If the care went beyond one week, we headed to the sheep camp right after school on Friday afternoon, where we spent the weekend, returning to the relative's home on Sunday evening. Evelyn said dad always bought groceries for our care provider.

Right Place, Right Time

There were at least four different camps we used during the spring and winter months. Those camps had permanent buildings that provided cooking, sleeping, and storage facilities as more people were there helping with various tasks. Two of these locations were used during the winter months as the houses provided protection from the cold. There were also permanent corrals and other resources that were needed in the spring as the herd was usually broken down into smaller groups during these two seasons.

The earliest camp where I spent part of the summer was at my paternal grandparents' sheep camp located about ten miles east of Guishche. At the time dad still had his herd with his brothers, Ross, Ralph, and Cecil. It was at this camp where I spent the most time being around them.

It was Cecil, the youngest brother, who spent much more time with us. He and dad had their sheep together later on, and they were particularly close. This was also the time when I was still too young to be assigned a herd to look after. Later, Uncle Cecil gave up his herd in order to join his family in Utah, where his wife was working. However, he often came home to visit, oftentimes staying with dad for periods of time at the sheep camp.

The second camp where my family spent at least one summer was located further east from the Carr family camp. This camp belonged to a family with whom dad had his sheep that particular summer. I especially remember this camp which was located in a small canyon. It was really hot there because it was located in such a sheltered place.

The two other summer camps where I spent the most summers are located within three or four miles of each other. The one I refer to as Yagach'a is located at the western edge of the sloping red-colored mesa. This parallels Interstate 40 on the north side, East and West of the New Mexico State Road 6 Exit. Yagach'a refers to the red sandstone rock that borders the mesa.

Chapter 4 Early Years as a Sheep Herder

Yagach'a
My Summer Home

Ruins of Great Grandfather Felipe Sarracino's Sheep Camp
Photo Taken by Rhiannon Carr

Right Place, Right Time

Skro kana is the name of the other location where my great grandfather, Felipe, had his sheep camp. His house is located right on the north bank of the San Jose River. About a quarter mile north of his house is the newer camp owned by my grandparents and used by my dad. It's located southwest of Yagach'a, and the Santa Fe Railroad track lies about midway between them.

Grandparents' Sheep Camp at Skro kana

At the time my story takes place, the construction of Interstate 40 had not yet reached this far west, and U. S. Route 66 was the two lane interstate highway at the time. Just east of where Highway 6 exits, U. S. Route 66 began veering to the Southwest, forming an arching route to and past the Laguna village of Mesita. Great grandfather Felipe's camp was located a few hundred yards north of this Highway, about midway between the Highway 6 Exit and the village of Mesita.

Before I was assigned a herd to look after, I would occasionally walk the three miles to visit my grandmother at

Chapter 4 Early Years as a Sheep Herder

Skro kana, returning home by late afternoon. There were times I and my other siblings actually lived with her for short periods of time both at her sheep camp and at Guishsche. All of us were very close to our grandmother. To get to her camp and back to Yagach'a I only had to cross the railroad tracks, as I-40 did not exist at the time.

The passing passenger and freight trains broke the monotony of sheep herding. A fence kept the sheep off the railroad tracks. I can still hear the sound of the train blowing its whistle, thinking it was acknowledging us. We always counted the number of cars being pulled, and sometimes we saw men sitting on the floor of the open box cars with their feet dangling outside.

One of the things we liked to do was to place pennies on the tracks. We would mark the spot by placing a marker on the side of the track so we could find the flattened pennies. Later when we began lambing and shearing at Skro kana, our sheep herding moved to the south side of the tracks.

It was at these two sheep camps that I saw and experienced the hard work that is involved in raising sheep for a living. I also witnessed how hard mom and dad worked to make a living for us.

Their work began each day way before sunrise as mother began preparing breakfast for us, while dad was out checking on the sheep which were corralled in several different places away from the house. He would be checking to see if any lambs were born overnight, and if an animal, such as a coyote or a bobcat, had gotten into any of the corrals during the night. Due to the increased workload during the lambing and shearing seasons, dad generally had to get extra help. This placed an additional burden on mother, who had to prepare all the meals for us.

As soon as dad returned from checking on the sheep, the day would begin for the rest of us. My sound sleep would suddenly be interrupted by his gentle voice saying, "Sah mudi, tro ipiti", my son, get up! By the way, the voice was no longer gentle-sounding

Right Place, Right Time

after about the second command to get up. When his tone changed I knew we had to get out from under the warm covers.

After a warm breakfast of either porridge made of ground corn, (hayani*), oatmeal, eggs, or leftover food from the day before, we headed to the corrals where the herds were penned. During the lambing season the entire herd was divided up into several groups, each requiring at least one herder. There were those expecting lambs, those not expecting to produce, those with newborns, and those ewes with older lambs.

One of the first tasks each morning was separating the ewes with the newborns from the herd of expecting ewes. Walter and I were responsible for herding the ones with the newborns. As the newborns became stronger they were moved to another herd.

Sometimes ewes rejected their young. In an attempt to get the mother to accept its young, the ewe and her newborn were placed in a small enclosure. If the mother still didn't accept the lamb, it was fed from a bottle.

Mother prepared lunches for all the herders. She even prepared one for Walter and me even though we didn't take the small herd very far from the house. She would wrap the lunch in a dish-towel which we rolled up, and then one of us would tie it around his waist.

Once, to break the monotony of having to be out looking after the sheep all day, Walter and I ate our lunch early, washed out the containers with the water from the canteens and went home for lunch. I don't think we've ever lived that one down as "real" sheep herders remained with their flock the entire day without going home for lunch. They didn't wash their containers either.

Daniel was responsible for herding the yearlings which required much closer oversight than the other sheep as they tended to roam a great deal more. One day a large number of them separated from the rest of the herd when Daniel was herding them.

Chapter 4 Early Years as a Sheep Herder

Dad had to get involved in the search for them. They were able to find all of them, to the relief of Dan and the rest of us sheep herders. He almost damaged our reputations as herders.

Evelyn and Daniel were herding one day when they saw a Roadrunner. They were able to get close enough to the bird that Dan threw his Levi jacket at it. The jacket landed on the bird. They caught it and took it back to the house with the intentions of keeping it for a pet. Mother made them release it in respect for an uncle's family who belonged to the Roadrunner Clan (Shaasrk'a* Hanu). We also caught baby rabbits. We quit catching them as they were never able to survive.

Evelyn was always one of the "herders". I don't recall her ever staying at the house with mother. My memories of her are mostly being out with us herding sheep. We found many ways to entertain ourselves during the course of the day. The two activities that provided the most fun were looking for arrowheads and bird nests, and counting the number of bird eggs we found in the nests.[11] For some reason, Yagach'a was one place where we found a lot of arrowheads and bird nests.

Sheepherding is extremely hard work. The days were hot, herding required constant walking, and the days were long. During one particular year, we had sand storms almost daily, which lasted from sunrise to sunset. In the mornings we would see the horizon already the shade of brown, a sign of another day of blowing sand. In the mornings our eyelids were crusted over, and mother had to use a damp cloth to soften the crust in order for us to open our eyes.

These types of days made no difference about the day's task of herding sheep. My parents got us goggles to protect our eyes from the blowing sand. We looked like open-cockpit pilots, wearing straw hats.

Each day we took the sheep out of the corrals usually by the time the sun was barely peeking over the horizon. We didn't corral

Right Place, Right Time

them until just before sunset. Even as young as we were, we spent about twelve hours a day walking. This was long before anyone thought about Day Light Savings Time. We didn't worry about the conservation of electricity or gas at that time. All we thought about was how best to conserve our own energy, such as finding a cedar tree under which we could sit and hope that the sheep wouldn't run off.

Dad generally took responsibility for looking after one of the herds, usually the ones that were still expecting lambs. I can still picture him as he was herding, walking with his upper body bent slightly forward. He would be walking slowly around the edge of his grazing flock with his shepherd's cane resting horizontally across his back with both arms hooked over the cane.

As his herd began to wander he would shout this one particular sound, and the sheep would pause, turn around to see where the sound was coming from, then either turn around, or remain where they were. He always carried a rattle made from a large coffee can that contained pebbles. The opening was flattened, and the handle consisted of several strands of wire attached to the can. He rattled the can to move the flock, or again, to stop them from wandering off.

If he had enough help, he "supervised" the herders. He would spend the day going from one herd to another making sure everything was in order. One of the major problems we encountered was rattlesnakes biting the sheep. They were always bitten on the face, and the face would swell up, so we were able to spot them right away. Dad would cut a slit under the jaws, squeeze out the venom, and spit his tobacco juice on the wound. I don't think he ever lost a sheep with his brand of treatment.

Another treatment was a liniment they called Kawaayu* waawa*, or horse medicine. Elgin may have been joking when he told me he thought they called it that as the bottle it came in had a

Chapter 4 Early Years as a Sheep Herder

picture of a horse on it. Anyway this liniment was used as a multi-purpose medicine for various wounds and infections suffered by the livestock.

My father loved his sheep, and he looked after them and cared for them almost like he loved and cared for his children. No kidding. He seemed to know every single one of his sheep, which numbered several hundred. During the course of the day we novice sheepherders had to count them periodically to make sure none were missing while dad would not only know immediately if one was missing, he'd know exactly which one it was.

He was demanding in how his herd was cared for. Some of the help would say he was too hard on us and on them and expected too much from us. We did work hard, but it was always accompanied with the loving support from both mom and dad. They never asked us to do anything that they knew we could not handle. As strict as he was about everything, he allowed us to learn to drive his truck when we were still very young. I believe all our driver education classes took place at the sheep camp and were given by an unlicensed instructor, dad.

We were evidently used to his expectations as we never saw it as being unreasonable. Dad didn't allow us to take comic books with us when we were herding. This now makes sense as the sheep tended to wander off very easily. It was especially so when the pods on the yucca plants began maturing. The sheep, and particularly the goats, would run from one plant to another for the pods.

Anyway, we were always so happy to see the sun reach the one inch mark above the western horizon. We would extend one arm in front of us to measure the distance the sun was above the horizon using our thumb and forefinger. At the one inch mark it was time to corral the herd.

After we corralled the herds in the evenings, we would return to the house and mother would always greet us with her

Right Place, Right Time

usual phrase, "Amu uh, wehs tda aku", a phrase of endearment welcoming us home. She would also have dinner ready. After washing up, we were more than ready to eat a hearty meal at a long table sitting on long benches. Mealtimes were fun. We'd talk about some of the things we did that day, and everybody at the table usually joined in the storytelling.

Sah Naya at Sheep Camp

After supper, we would show each other the arrowheads and report the number of nests and bird eggs we had found that day. Tabulating the arrowheads was easy as they were in our possession, although we occasionally had to ask dad whether some of our findings were legitimate. The "crediting" of the nests and bird eggs was harder as we had to describe the location where we found them in order not to duplicate each other's findings. Sometimes we pouted or cried if our findings and reports were questioned or were rejected outright.

We didn't stay up much beyond the time it got dark as we'd all walked miles that day. I do remember at Skro kana, sitting outside after it began to get dark, that we would see car lights slowly

Chapter 4 Early Years as a Sheep Herder

moving on U. S. Route 66. There weren't that many cars on the road at the time, and people didn't drive very fast as the cars didn't have that capability. When we saw a set of car lights, it seemed like forever before we saw another set of lights come over the horizon.

Most of us generally slept outdoors in the open or sometimes in a tent. It was fun sleeping out in the open as it was cool. We were able to see the shining stars, even if it was only for the few minutes we stayed awake. After what seemed like only a few minutes of sleep, we were awakened to that familiar refrain, "Sah mudi, tro ipiti."

Once the ewes had all their lambs it was time for the sheep to be sheared of their wool. Earlier on they were sheared by hand-manipulated shears. Later electric clippers powered by fuel generators were used. This was much faster, and it reduced the number of cuts inflicted on the sheep.

Each shearer was allotted a certain number of twine that was used to bundle the wool, as well as keeping a tally on the number each sheared as they were paid by the head. When the allotment was used up, he was issued the same number of twine. The shearing was done by an off-reservation team of men that traveled throughout the reservation working for the various sheep owners.

While shearing time was also busy, the work was less intense than the lambing season. It generally took less than a week for the entire herd to be sheared after the introduction of electric clippers. Mother, most times with help, had to feed all the herders, the shearers, along with others who were helping out. This time was exciting for the children as there was a slight change to the daily routine. It was fun watching the men shear, and in the evenings there would be a lot of people around.

Small groups of sheep were corralled at a time in order to reduce the number that would be kept from grazing. Generally

Right Place, Right Time

there were about three or four men doing the shearing. Each would grab a sheep by its hind leg and with the other hand grab the sheep on top of the neck and steer it to a wooden platform several inches off the ground. The platform helped keep the dirt from getting into the wool. Above the platform was stretched a tarp to shield the shearers from the sun.

Once the sheep was laid on the platform, its legs were bound with a short rope and the shearing would begin. To shear one head generally took, maybe about twenty minutes. As soon as one was sheared, the wool was gathered up and tied in a bundle with twine and placed in a large five or six foot burlap sack that hung inside a wooden frame specifically built for this purpose. A person would stand inside the sack to tamp down the bundles of wool as they were tossed in the sack. When the sack was filled, the opening was stitched with wire, and it took several men to remove the sack from the frame

After the shearing was completed, the wool was hauled to the trader with whom my father conducted practically all of his business. The money brought in by selling the wool produced about one half of the family's annual income. This income was used to pay off the debts the family had accumulated for the purchases of groceries, livestock feed, clothing, and loans that dad had gotten from the trader for his children's boarding school tuition.

This was also the time my parents were able to make additional purchases such as clothing, shoes, or new straw hats for us. We looked forward to these sales, as well as any trips to the store as our parents always bought us treats like chewing gum, cracker jacks, and always fresh fruit.

Often times the adult men would get inebriated when the wool was sold. Unfortunately, our dad took part in it. One or two would get more inebriated than the others. The drinking did not extend beyond that one day so it was over with pretty quickly.

Chapter 4 Early Years as a Sheep Herder

My mother loathed drinking, so it did produce tensions between my parents that lasted beyond that day. This drinking put a damper on what was generally a happy event as the most difficult part of raising sheep had come to an end for the year. Drinking in that particular era could never be described as social drinking. Even today any type of drinking remains one of the least acceptable and most damaging behaviors in our family.

Once the shearing was over, the next two tasks were the removal the tails of the lambs and the castration of most of the male lambs. Both of these procedures were initially performed manually with a knife. Later on, the tails were removed and the male lambs castrated using heavy rubber bands which were wound tightly around the appendages to be removed. I'm not sure exactly why the tails were removed other than to keep from collecting burrs.

We once cared for an orphaned lamb whose tail was never removed. It grew long enough to drag it on the ground, and it did collect a lot of burrs. The poor lamb also looked weird with the long tail. When dad was still performing "surgery" with his knife, he would build a small fire. He would toss into the fire the tails, which had a little meat on them and testicles to roast for us to eat.

After these additional tasks were completed, generally around the end of May or early June, it was time to take the herd to the higher elevations on the reservation where there were generally greener pastures and cooler temperatures. This move from the lambing and shearing site brought a number of changes. Mother and the youngest of the family returned home, and dad and others moved with the herd to the new grazing area. As I grew older I became involved in these moves.

There were two general areas on the reservation where the herd was relocated. One was on the eastern most mesa of the reservation, east of Guishsche. On this mesa stands a lone rock formation named Bell Rock that is big enough to be seen from afar.

Right Place, Right Time

Daniel and I played a lot on the top of this formation while we were herding. The area to which the herd was moved depended on the availability of feed for the sheep.

Jack Ward, the second area where we took the herd, was more controlled in terms of its use by herders. The number of herds that were allowed on this land was restricted. The herds were also assigned to specific areas for grazing, and the camp sites had to be moved about every three days, preventing overgrazing.

Jack Ward is located at the southwestern edge of the reservation, south of the Sky City of Acoma at an elevation close to 7000 feet above sea level. At this level it was much cooler, with Ponderosa pine and generally a lot of feed for the sheep. Jack Ward was where we saw orioles for the first time. Their sac-like nests hung from the branches of the ponderosa pine trees.

It was one of these moves from the lambing and shearing site to Jack Ward that I participated in as a youngster. We must have completed the lambing/shearing season on the mesa on which Bell Rock is located as it was from this mesa that we moved the herd. The distance to Jack Ward is approximately twenty five to thirty five miles from the starting point. We used donkeys for moving the camping gear and supplies.

We began moving the herd before sunrise, and they had to be moved down a steep trail at the southern edge of the mesa. One of the goats led the flock down the trail. Even though the herd was on constant move, they had to graze along the way. The move took at least three days to drive the sheep to Jack Ward. The last night we camped at the base of the mesa on which Jack Ward is located.

Again before sunrise of the final morning we began moving the herd up the trail with a goat taking the lead. I can't recall how long it took to get the herd up to the top. I do remember how cool it was after we reached the top, and I still remember the sound of the breeze blowing through the ponderosa pines. One thing I'll always

Chapter 4 Early Years as a Sheep Herder

remember about this trek to the top was the rattlesnakes that blended in with the color of the dark grey rock. The ones found in this area were not necessarily long, however their girths were big.

Once we got the herd to Jack Ward the daily routines became much more relaxed as we now had only one herd to look after. Too, grass was more plentiful, and the sheep didn't roam as much in search of vegetation. We moved the camp using donkeys from one site to another about every three days; the move was often less than a mile. The herd was not corralled at night, and they never roamed away from the camp unless something scared them.

During the day as it began to get warm, the herd gathered under the trees, and we would enjoy a leisurely lunch at the campsite and even a short nap afterward. Dad would always open a can of something sweet for dessert, such as fruit cocktail, pears, or peaches. Sometimes he would open a can of whole tomatoes to which we would add sugar to sweeten them. As the day began to cool, the sheep began moving out from under the trees to begin grazing again.

Toward the end of the day dad would send us back to the camp to build the camp fire to get it ready for cooking. He did all the cooking for us, using the Dutch oven for most of his cooking. This included baking biscuits. Cooked mutton produced a lot of grease, and we would dip our bread in the drippings. My mouth still waters when I think of these meals. After eating we'd sit around the fire. Sometimes we would collect the powder from dead pine trees and throw it in the fire to make it sparkle.

We rarely stayed up very long as we were usually pretty tired by evening. We slept inside a tent as the nights were much cooler. Dad woke us up after he had breakfast ready for us in the morning. At the sheep camp he allowed us to drink coffee, but we never drank it at home. I don't know why. It possibly had to do with the need to

Right Place, Right Time

warm up as it was always cold in the mornings. The coffee, with a lot of evaporated milk and sugar in it, tasted great.

One time Evelyn and Daniel spent the entire summer with dad at Jack Ward. Evelyn thought it was unusual for dad to let her. Dan had wanted her to stay, she thought because he didn't want to stay by himself. One time the two of them removed all the labels from their supply of canned foods, never knowing what an opened can would produce. I imagine Dad didn't like it at the time, but I'm sure he and mom got a laugh out of it later as they tended to do. Years later someone asked Daniel if he wanted to accompany them on a camping trip. He declined, saying that his sheep camp days had provided him with enough camping experiences.

The time spent at Jack Ward was the last phase of my sheep herding for the year because by August we returned home to get ready for school. Dad remained there with the sheep for another month, and then he returned the herd back to the summer camp where he would keep them for the winter and spring.

In about October the lambs were sold. The selling of the lambs brought in the second and the last installment of my parents' annual income. Again, the lambs were sold to the same trader who bought his wool. Whether the money from sales of his wool and lambs was enough to pay off his debts incurred during the course of the year, I don't know. Since he was able to get credit for his purchases for his family, he always dealt with this same trader. The next time any income would be coming in for my family would be the following spring from the sale of the wool.

Draught Takes Family to Oklahoma

There was one summer that was completely different for us. This change came as a result of a severe drought around 1949 or 1950. The federal government arranged for the tribal sheep growers to transport their herds to grazing areas at several locations: Eastern

Chapter 4 Early Years as a Sheep Herder

New Mexico, the Tyrone, Oklahoma area in the Panhandle, and near Stratford, Oklahoma, east of Oklahoma City. A number of sheep growers took advantage of this opportunity, including my father.

I don't know if the stockmen were given a choice as to where to take their herds, but dad and one of his brothers took their herds to Stratford. This provided us an opportunity to spend a summer, I believe in 1950, in hot and humid rural Oklahoma. This was our first experience with this type of climate, and the first time we left the reservation to live elsewhere for a period of time. Not only did we suffer from the humidity, but we also suffered from chigger bites, another first time experience with these pesky insects.

This time in Oklahoma presented us with a whole array of new experiences. We lived in a frame house that must have been on the land the government had leased for us. It was not very far southwest of the small farm community of Stratford. The houses we saw, including the one we lived in, had siding that made them look like brick homes, which I thought they were until I was told otherwise.

The water came from a well outside the house, and if I remember correctly, I think the water was brought to the surface in a long cylinder container. There was a cellar out in the yard that we were told was a shelter from tornadoes, which we had the good fortune not to experience.

The mail was delivered to a rural mailbox located a short distance from the house. Walter and I watched for the mailman to come down the road, and if he stopped at our mail box, we would run down to pick up the mail. We learned that the flag on the mailbox had to be raised for the mail man to stop and pick up the mail. I remember writing a letter to my friend, Phillip, from home and anxiously awaiting his reply just to experience getting a letter by such a different system. At home, the post office was in a private residence by the plaza.

Right Place, Right Time

Wild turtles were new to us as the only kind I had previously seen had American flag decals on their backs, the dime store variety. I will never forget scratching the surface of a moist creek bed with a stick and seeing water seep from the ground. This experience was impressive. Knee high grass we had never seen before. Walter and I also learned to fish from a pond.

We had neighbors who lived down the road from us who we thought were a Black family. We learned later they were an Indian family from one of the local tribes. They were much darker in complexion than we were. At the time I didn't know there were Indians in Oklahoma, or for that matter, anyplace else.

One evening we drove into Stratford to buy groceries. As we were coming into town I pointed out a sign on a building that must have said Cherry's. I must have thought it was advertising the fruit. My mother told dad to stop so we could buy some cherries. Nobody in the truck caught the error until we went into the store to purchase cherries. The incident did not embarrass my parents, and they were able to laugh about it.

As I think back to this summer experience in Oklahoma, I marvel at how brave and self-confident my parents were. They had never been this far away from the reservation, yet they were willing to go to this faraway place where they didn't know anyone. Even driving to Oklahoma for the first time, a distance of over five hundred miles would be challenging during that time. Daniel thought we just camped out at night on the side of the highway on the way to Stratford. I don't recall much about the drive to Oklahoma. I do remember our return, with the exception of camping at night, which we must have done.

I remember the names of some of the towns we drove through, such as Hollis, Oklahoma, and Wildorado and Bushland, Texas, the latter two being just tiny communities with gas stations, west of Amarillo. The back of our truck was loaded up to the cab

Chapter 4 Early Years as a Sheep Herder

level, and Daniel and our cousin, Joyce Ann, and I sat on top of the load all the way back to Guishsche. Years later, we talked about how we must have resembled the people migrating to California during the Depression.

One of the often used tribal expressions is Imii'i and Imi'i, male and female expressions of fear or reluctance. Although my parents used this expression a lot, they never seemed to be intimidated by much. Just as I got a lot of my confidence from them, they must have received it from their families.

Returning to School

We always got home from the sheep camp, and even from Oklahoma, in time for school. Those already enrolled at Ganado didn't have to return until after Labor Day. By that time Walter and I were already back in the local day school.

Preparation for school involved shopping for school clothes. One year Edna took Walter and me to purchase shoes. I bought a pair of shoes that had tire tread-like soles that I really liked, even though they were a size larger than what fitted me. I didn't tell Edna that they were too big, but I had to stuff wads of paper in the shoes when I started wearing them. Mother purchased most of our clothes ordering by mail from her favorite stores, Sears or Montgomery Wards, using their catalogs. What was purchased for us in preparation for the new school year was pretty limited, but pre-school shopping was a big event for us.

Looking back to this period, I've often wondered how my parents were able to manage, with their limited income, for their family of eight children. We always had plenty of food, such as mutton from the sheep and the produce from the gardens. We always had two sets of clothes, one for play and the other for school and special occasions. We were like most of the other families in the village. There was a family or two that were better off than most.

Right Place, Right Time

As we grew older, we were able to help out a little, such as when we stayed at the Mission to work for the following year's tuition. While there were things I could not buy, such as a letter jacket, our parents were always able to provide us the essentials of food, shelter, and clothing, and some extras when they were able.

Chapter 5
Education of My Early Relatives

I suspect that the importance of education in my family grew out of the fact that at least nine of my parents' immediate family members were educated at Carlisle. The school had recruited quite heavily in the West, rounding up Indian children that included these relatives and many others from Laguna. These children were basically shipped to Carlisle, over two thousand miles away.

From 1879 until 1918, over 10,000 Native American children from 140 tribes attended Carlisle
Photo and caption from Wikipedia
"Carlisle Indian Industrial School",
http://en.wikipedia.org/wiki/Carlisle_Indian_Industrial_School
November 2, 2013

It was not until 1881 that a boarding school that was closer to our reservation was opened by the Presbyterian Church in Duranes, New Mexico Territory. This school was turned over to the government in 1886, becoming the Albuquerque Indian School.[12]

Right Place, Right Time

By then, some of my relatives were already at Carlisle. Both of my parents must have seen the benefits of an education from these relatives. My mother's side of the family showed more clearly what a person could accomplish with an education.

Her two aunts, Ayche and Etta Sarracino, became trained nurses. Ayche was a nurse at the Indian hospital when Elgin was born there. She was also a Post Mistress at Guishsche. Their brother, John Sarracino, served several terms as Governor of the tribe. He was an interpreter in the Presbyterian Church, and he also ran the local store for the owner. Their other brother, Josiah, worked for the Santa Fe Railroads in Winslow, Arizona, eventually retiring to his ranch in the southwestern part of the reservation.

Photograph of Hudson from the
American Indian Athletic Hall of Fame
Wikipedia November 3, 2013
http://en.wikipedia.org/wiki/Frank_Hudson_(American_football)

Chapter 5 Education of My Early Relatives

On my father's side, Frank Hudson, the All American football player, did not return home to live. He remained in the East after he left Carlisle. He lived out his years in Pennsylvania where he worked in the banking sector. I learned about his football exploits at Carlisle, and afterward, from reading Sally Jenkins' book, *The Real All Americans*,[13] and Lars Anderson's *Carlisle vs. Army*.[14]

Mr. Hudson and one of his brothers may have been the only ones on my father's side of the family who were ever employed in the private or public sector. My paternal grandparents continued to raise sheep for their livelihood after their stint at Carlisle.

I believe the experiences these relatives brought home gave my parents a glimpse of what was possible with an education. Other factors may have entered into our parents' belief that education was a must for their children.

Neither of them had much schooling. They did want us to be well prepared for our independence. Daniel said he was always encouraged by dad to remain in school so that he wouldn't have to end up herding sheep for a living because it was such hard work. I don't think college attendance was ever a stated goal as I do not recall it ever being discussed at home.

All of us chose to go on to get some type of training after high school. As late as the mid 1950's, the only persons I knew who were in college from Guishsche were my sister, Evelyn, and one of her high school classmates. There may have been some from the other villages.

The Carlisle school did play a large part in my family's and tribe's educational history. Many stories are told about the returning English-speaking Carlisle students. One I remember went something like this: A returning student asked, pointing to one of. our mud-plastered houses, "Whose dis chicken house?" In Laguna, the person being asked responded with, "What do you mean chicken house. That is your uncle so and so's house!"

Right Place, Right Time

What remains today of the tribe's Carlisle connections are the existence of three clusters of houses located near the Village of Seama. They are named after Eastern cities students became familiar with while going to school at Carlisle. These clusters of homes are named Philadelphia, Harrisburg, and New York. They still go by those names today

Chapter 6
My Education Begins
1945 - 1952

Paguate Day School

The beginnings of the formal education for all eight of the Pedro and Edith Pacheco Carr children began at the Paguate Day School, the local government-operated elementary school. Kathryn, the eldest of the Carr children, entered the day school as a beginner in about 1932 or 1933. Seven of us followed her, the last ones leaving in 1952.

My educational journey began in the late summer of 1946 as a beginner. There are only a few things I remember about my elementary school days. The most important was the fact that we had to start learning how to speak and write in English. Our primary language before starting school was Laguna, so all of us were in the same boat.

One of the teachers was my grandmother's sister-in-law, John Sarracino's wife. There were many times at the beginning of our schooling that she had to explain things to us in Laguna when we didn't understand what she was trying to tell us in English. I'm told that the first sentence I ever wrote was, "May I take off my pants?"

We all went home for lunch as this was decades before school lunch programs were initiated. The beginners were also required to take naps in the afternoon on mats laid out between rows of desks. I don't know if any of us ever went to sleep as most of us were never allowed to do so at home during the day.

During my time there, the day school allowed the children time off for religious instruction. A Protestant minister and a Catholic priest came to the school to conduct classes for the children "belonging" to their respective churches. There were only a few

Right Place, Right Time

children in the Protestant group other than the Carrs, as the villagers were predominantly Roman Catholic.

At the end of the school year we always went on a school picnic. One year was particularly memorable. My friend, Phillip, and I transported our school mates to the picnic site in two horse drawn wagons that belonged to our grandfathers. Not all of them could fit into the wagons, so some had to walk.

What made this particular outing noteworthy was that as we were leaving the village, one of the wagons got too close to the edge of the dirt road, and one of the wheels went into an irrigation ditch. We had to unload everyone so we could push the wagon to get the one wheel out of the ditch. Each of us was responsible for taking our own food, and boiled eggs seemed pretty popular. We probably had Kool Aid as it was the common refreshment of that time.

In 1952, Walter, our youngest brother and I left for boarding school. He had completed his third grade year, and I had completed the sixth grade. Our departures ended the Carr children's twenty year presence at the Paguate Day School. As far as I know, there were only one or two other families who had children attending the school for about as long as the Carr children did.

Why were all the Carr children able to complete this first segment of their formal schooling successfully? The primary reason was that mother never let us miss school. Dad was just as adamant. He could have very easily used his perennial need for help with the care of his sheep as a reason for keeping the boys out of school. He needed the most help at the start of the lambing season, yet he made sure we finished the school year. He also made sure we got home at the end of the summer to get ready to return to school.

Another example of our father's commitment to our schooling was that he was forever having to arrange for loans in order to pay for our tuition. He even sold and traded some of his property in order to pay for our schooling, according to one of my

Chapter 6 My Education Begins

sisters. If I remember correctly, the annual tuition was $100.00, and there were four of us in school at the same time.

Our parents always pointed out to us how hard it was raising sheep for a living as a way of encouraging us to remain in school. All of us knew firsthand how hard it was as that's what we did every summer, so I always looked forward to returning to school in the fall.

"Graduation" from the Paguate Day School after completing the sixth grade meant that the "graduates", except for a few, would be leaving home the following August for various boarding schools away from the reservation. Most would be going to the Albuquerque Indian School. A few would go to St. Catherine's School in Santa Fe or to the Santa Fe Indian School.

Walter and I knew we were going to Ganado. I don't think we were afraid of going as Evelyn and Daniel were still going to be there. Besides, all my older siblings liked it there. However, this separation meant that we would be leaving a life that had been pretty safe and secure to another setting that would bring about a different way of life without our parents. Leaving home to attend boarding school was expected, and at the time I did not seem to be fearful of the unknown.

Break Up of Family

Our family, as well as most Indian families, was no longer intact by the time we reached the age of twelve, or younger. During this period, most of us were already living in boarding schools by that age. Exceptions of course were those whose families were already living off the reservations, or living within a public school district.

Once my siblings and I left home, the most time any of us spent at home was during the summer months. By the time we got to high school age, most of us began spending all or portions of the summers working away from home. Therefore, our parents only had direct everyday oversight of us for the first ten to twelve years, and

Right Place, Right Time

our adolescent years were spent under the care and direction of others.

My generation did not have to attend boarding schools as far away as my early relatives did when they were sent to Carlisle, Pennsylvania. However, the parent-child separation issues remained the same. I cannot imagine the pain involved if I had to see my son, at the age of five or six, being taken about two thousand miles away and not knowing when I would see him again.

However, during my time it was still the government's policies that placed us in boarding schools. At least my siblings and I were able to come home during the Christmas holidays and summers. Mom and dad were also able to come to visit us once in a great while, sometimes staying overnight in one of the cottages the Mission maintained for visitors.

So the Carr family and their early relatives, along with all the other tribal children, suffered the effects of these early forced separations due to the government's Indian education policies. I will have to refer you to other literature to learn of the effects of early separation of children from their families and the impact these boarding schools had on Indian families throughout history. This story will only talk about my experiences and what my sisters and brothers have shared with me.

My Brief Stop
at the
Albuquerque Indian
School
abqjournal.com
11/24/13

Chapter 7
Boarding School Years
1952 - 1958

Attending a boarding school was basically the only option we had for going on to high school after we completed the sixth grade at the Paguate Day School. Like all of our older siblings, Walter and I knew Ganado would be our destination. Ganado is about 150 miles from home.

At least it wasn't as far as Carlisle, Pennsylvania. Still, Ganado was quite a ways from home, and my parents were dependent on others to drive us to and from school. Later we did get a vehicle so dad was able to transport us. I don't recall dreading going away to boarding school as it was a natural part of growing up in our family.

Brief Stop en Route to Ganado

By the time I was all set to leave for Ganado there was no room for me there in the fall of 1952. As a result, I entered the Albuquerque Indian School in August, along with most of my day school classmates. Walter would be accompanying Evelyn and Daniel as they were returning for their 11th and 9th grade years, respectively. Walter was being admitted as a 4th grader. He was ten years of age at the time. I'm assuming that my parents decided to send him away to school at his young age since Evelyn and Daniel would be there to look after him.

I left for the Indian school while the three remained at home awaiting the beginning of their school year, which began and ended later than the government boarding schools. The Indian school used to send out a bus to pick up the students at the beginning of the school year. I may have accompanied the other Indian school-bound

Right Place, Right Time

students. More likely, my sister Edna and my future brother-in-law probably took me since they both lived in Albuquerque. Practically all my classmates from Paguate Day School entered the Albuquerque Indian School with me, but I really got lonesome, despite the fact that Edna only lived a few blocks from the campus.

There were a number of things that fueled this homesickness in addition to being cut off from my family for the first time in my life. Memories of my short stay at the school are highlighted by the threatening nature of the school environment and its personnel. I remember being supervised by unsmiling, always threatening, Indian personnel, who seemed always quick to threaten punishment if we didn't do what they directed.

As I look back, the personnel who stood out in this manner, I'm assuming, were long time government employees as bureaucracies tend to perpetuate these types of attitudes. My surprise was that it was Indian adults who were treating us in this manner. Sadly, this condescending attitude on the part of many public employees remains as true today as it was in the 1950's.

I got so homesick that my sister, Edna, must have felt sorry for me. She let me stay with her at her apartment. I don't know if I begged her or cried. Whichever I did, it worked, as she took me in. I walked the few blocks from her apartment to school for the few more days I remained there. Thank goodness, a bed became available at Ganado, and I was able to join Evelyn, Daniel, and Walter. My stay at AIS was brief and painful.

I've often wondered if I would have gone on to college if I had remained at the Indian School. Many of their graduates ended up going to Haskell Institute, a government post high school vocational school located in Lawrence, Kansas, or they entered other government sponsored programs. Vocational training was still the government's Indian education policy although Haskell eventually became a junior college.

Chapter 7 Boarding School Years

I did not know that Evelyn also attended the Albuquerque Indian School for the same reason that I did. She evidently stayed longer as she remembered making a wash stand out of a wooden crate in one of her classes. When she got to the Mission, she was behind in the school courses and had to work hard to catch up with her new school mates.

She said dad didn't really want her to transfer as she had at least "gotten used to" the Indian school. I'm glad he relented as she may not have ever gone on to college either if she had remained. I guess at that time the government didn't feel we had any potential for college level work so that all it basically offered was vocational training in their schools.

Even though I eventually went to work for the Bureau of Indian Affairs, one of my life long resentments against the agency was its failure and resistance to acknowledge the capabilities and potential of Indians. I've always believed that those students who continued their training at Haskell Institute could have easily succeeded in college. While I'm willing to give the government schools credit for turning out graduates with sound vocational skills, it did not do a whole lot to encourage its graduates to go on to college.

This policy prevented many students of my generation from getting the schooling to enter the professions, such as medicine, engineering, etc. Many of my classmates and friends who ended up at vocational schools had as much or more potential than I had to succeed in college.

Ganado Mission

The Mission was founded in 1901 "by an "expeditionary force" representing the Presbyterian National Board of Home Missions. Their task was to locate a desirable site for a mission to serve the Navajo Indians. The party settled on a site less than a mile

Right Place, Right Time

east of the Hubbell Trading Post, which is now designated as a National Historic Site, on the Navajo Reservation in Northeastern Arizona.

A manse was built on the site of the current Ganado Mission that served as the home for the first missionary and his wife. The manse also served as a meeting place and a classroom for the day school started by the missionary's wife. From this beginning, the Presbyterian Church's three-fold program of evangelism, education, and health care got underway.[15]

Ganado Mission Boarding School
Aerial Photograph
Taken 12/14/49 for Article
by Robert A. Barnes

By the time I arrived at the Mission fifty one years later in September, 1952, it already had a long and established history in the three service areas the Presbyterian Church envisioned in 1901. The

Chapter 7 Boarding School Years

Presbyterian Church ministered to its student body, its personnel, and to the Navajo people and others who lived in the surrounding area, led by an ordained minister and lay ministers. The Sage Memorial Hospital was serving patients in this region of the Navajo Reservation. An accredited school of nursing, which closed in 1951, was a part of the hospital.

The school accepted students in grades 4–12. Walter's fourth grade class may have been the last one to be admitted as the elementary school was phased out shortly after I got there. The Mission was pretty self-sustaining. It had its own well to supply the water, a power plant that provided the utilities for the campus, and a dairy farm which was also phased out during my stay.

Just prior to my arrival, the superintendent was the renowned missionary-physician, Clarence G. Salsbury, M.D. He was succeeded by Dr. Joseph Poncel, who was the Superintendent during my six years at the school. It was during the administrations of these two men that all eight Carr children got their high school educations. Our sister, Alice, attended and graduated from its Sage Memorial Hospital School of Nursing in 1949. The mission was supported by the Board of National Missions of the Presbyterian Church USA.

Happy to Get to Ganado

I must have arrived just before noon on a school day as I remember joining Walter and some of the boys waiting in the park for the dining hall to open for lunch. One of my recollections of that first day was the friendliness of the students, and I was especially impressed that Walter had already made friends. The school had a pretty campus, with green lawns and the little park with a pond between the dining hall and the church. I was immediately struck by how different this school was in comparison to the atmosphere I had just experienced at the Albuquerque Indian School.

Right Place, Right Time

Photo Originally in Color, Provided by Marilyn Dalton

The enrollment was around 200 students, grades 4-12 at the time. The students came from many different tribes. The Navajo Tribe had the largest representation, followed by the Hopis, then possibly my tribe. Some of the students came from Alaska, California, Oklahoma, and other western states.

All of us lived in dormitories, except the children of Mission employees who lived on campus. The exception was the son of one of the teachers who did live in the dormitory. Students in the 4th through the 9th grades lived in the dormitory located above the dining hall, and the 10th-12th graders lived in what had been the original high school building that had been converted into living quarters. This residence hall had individual rooms that housed three to five boys each, depending on the size of the rooms.

The girls had two dormitories that basically had the same housing patterns as the boys. The elementary school was located in one part of the first floor of one of the girl's dormitories.

Chapter 7 Boarding School Years

A "Work-Study" School

My use of the term is not exactly the way we use "Work-Study" today in describing an educational program that combines work and study. What we had may have been an earlier version of this model. I'm kidding. The entire Mission was operated by paid personnel, volunteers, and, yes, the student body. All the students were assigned jobs which were performed daily. The job assignment was governed by the age of the student.

For example, Walter's first job assignment was cleaning one set of staircases that led up to the boys' dormitory above the dining hall and kitchen. His job was sweeping the stairways every day, and on Saturday mornings, mopping them.   All our jobs supported practically all aspects of the daily operation of the school, including the operation of the farm until it was phased out.

My assignments during my six years were working in the kitchen, the bakery, the staff commissary, the kitchen pantry, the gym, and others I can't remember. I may have started off working in one section of the boy's dormitory, as I recall the fun we had trying to ride a big buffer which we used for the floors on Saturdays.

While we moaned and groaned about having to work, I actually believe most of us had fun. I did anyway. Some of the work assignments required the students to get up early, such as those who worked at "The Barn" milking the cows, etc., and in the kitchen.

The Carrs were used to working at home anyway, and I imagine most of the other students were too. We worked two hours a day, Monday through Friday, then all morning on Saturdays. We were off on Sundays, except for those who worked in "strategic positions", or as the government today would describe them, "essential personnel", such as those working in the dining room and the kitchen since we had to eat.

There was one Saturday in the spring that was designated as a clean-up day. The day was devoted to cleaning up the campus. I

Right Place, Right Time

remember it being a fun day, and our noon meal was not our regular beef and gravy meal. I have pictures of students with faces painted, wearing funny hats, and with yard tools in their hands.

Working in the kitchen provided the most opportunities for fun and a place to find extra things to eat. The kitchen was one place that had the most students working there at any one time, and with only one person being in charge made it very easy to take advantage of the situation.

One trick that I always remember was the time we mixed a few raw eggs in a bowl of boiled eggs that was set out at breakfast for staff members who ate in the dining hall. Word spread among the students that this was planned for this one morning. While trying to not to be so obvious about looking on the staff side of the dining hall, we couldn't keep from glancing over there to see the faces of the lucky ones who would be cracking the raw eggs. Sure enough we saw it happen! We all had a great laugh out of it, even the person and his table mates laughed.

We had a volunteer fire department manned by the students and staff. No, we did not have a motorized fire truck or a Dalmatian dog riding on our cart which carried a basic set of "firefighting" equipment. The cart also had to be pulled and pushed by the "firemen". We had fire drills, usually in the middle of the night, which we hated.

One time we did have an actual fire in the middle of the night across the wash, a dry river bed, from the campus. As I recall we "firemen" were either too late getting there with the cart, or there was no water available near the fire. We just stood and watched the fire burn. It was a lost opportunity to exhibit our firefighting skills.

I'm guessing that the work assignments were intended to teach us how to be responsible and accountable, and of course, to keep the campus functioning. The supervision and expectations

Chapter 7 Boarding School Years

were always reasonable and were carried out in a non-threatening manner, although some of the staff were stricter than others. Elgin said he spent a summer working at the Mission on the farm. He evidently didn't perform as was expected and said he was "removed from the job". I asked him if he was reassigned to another job. He laughed and said no, he was sent home.

The job I enjoyed the most was working in the gym as the work entailed doing different things. For example, during the football season the coach and I would spend Saturday mornings lining our dirt football field for the home games and removing bull heads. During the basketball season we were readying the gym for games and cleaning the gym the day following. Another big job was refinishing the gym floor in preparation for the new basketball season. My boss was a no-nonsense type of guy, and while we did not talk much, I enjoyed the work assignment.

Life in the Dorm

Other than the few days I spent in the Indian School dormitory, this was my first experience living in one. English was now our "full time" language. Native languages continued to be spoken within the tribal groups represented at the school.

Many former boarding school students have claimed they lost their tribal languages because they were not allowed to speak it. I imagine it was true particularly in government boarding schools as their philosophy was to acculturate the students, and one of their ways of doing it was to prohibit them from speaking their native languages. Judging from my experience at the Indian School, I'm sure the punishment would have been harsh. In addition, many students did not come home for long periods of time, such as those who went to Carlisle. I don't think there was a policy about not speaking our own languages. If such a policy existed, it was disregarded.

Right Place, Right Time

The friendly atmosphere of the school made my adjustment to my new surroundings easy, and I felt an immediate acceptance by the students and mission personnel. While there were many "firsts" for me, I got off to a good start. Walter and I began our boarding school life living in the same dormitory, and neither of us had any trouble adjusting to our new living situation.

There were three sections to the dormitory above the dining hall. One section was for the 4th-7th graders; another section for the 8th and 9th graders; and three small rooms that were assigned to six of the older students, me being one of them in my 9th grade year. Our daily schedules were pretty structured. Monday through Friday were school days. The day began at 6:00 in the mornings, breakfast at 7:00, and classes began at 8:00. During the course of the day we had to meet our daily two hour work obligations.

Monday, Tuesday, and Wednesday nights we had study hall from 7-8 in the high school building; Thursday nights were set aside for organizational activities; and one night a week after study hall we had devotions in the dorm living room which consisted of hymn singing, a prayer, and a lesson generally given by our housemother. She also played the piano, and boy did we belt out those hymns! Out of this experience I grew to appreciate the hymns we learned and sang. Even today I enjoy just listening to them as I've never developed a voice to do justice to singing them, or for that matter any song.

Most of the students came from modest homes like ours. We all brought a limited supply of clothing as well as money. What money we had, we withdrew from what the housemother kept for us in small manila envelopes with our names on it. I never had much in my envelope. We got occasional money from home which went for movies, snacks, and other small items.

There was a trading post and a small café across the road from the campus. Most of us really didn't have money to buy "eats",

Chapter 7 Boarding School Years

but when we did go to the trading post or café, we had to pin a small ribbon on our shirt to show we had permission to leave the campus. Some of the boys pinned their ribbons on the leg of their jeans.

The popular purchases were such things as a loaf of bread, a few slices of bologna, or a jar of hot yellow peppers which we were allowed to take into the dining hall to spice up our meals. Fortunately for most of us, french fries were the most affordable menu item from the café. There were a few students that were better off than others.

No evening meals were served in the dining hall on Sundays. "Dry sandwiches," mainly peanut butter and jelly sandwiches, and a piece of fruit, were prepared for us and delivered to our dorms. This is what we ate every Sunday evening throughout the years we spent at Ganado. Once a year a truck load of fresh grapefruit was hauled in from Phoenix, and for weeks we ate fresh grapefruit for dessert and snacks.

As might be expected of students living together, we found many ways to entertain ourselves. Sometimes we didn't go right off to sleep after the lights were turned off at bedtime. After most of our dorm mates had gone to sleep, a few of us used our artistic talents to paint the faces of the deep sleepers using liquid shoe polish. The following morning they saw themselves in the bathroom mirror with mustaches, black eyes, or beards. Short-sheeting was another favorite trick to play, but it worked best on those who were trying to get in bed quickly.

There was one activity that we engaged in that we evidently didn't realize how dangerous it was. Several of us would form a chain holding hands. The boy at one end would hold the chain that hung from a light fixture located above the sinks in the bathroom while the one at the opposite end touched or held a water faucet. We felt the electricity charge go through us.

Right Place, Right Time

Another pastime was skipping church on Sundays. There was a half-hour break between Sunday school and the church service, and we generally went back to the dormitory. Those who didn't want to go to church hid under the beds. We knew the housemother's routine during that break. As she was leaving for church she would walk through the dormitory to make sure everyone had left for church.

As soon as we heard the door shut at the bottom of the stairs, we began crawling out from under the beds, never knowing who and how many would crawl out. Eventually the housemother began missing some of her charges at church, and then we were assigned to specific pews.

We liked to sneak out of the dorm at night. One night two older boys and I snuck out after bedtime using the fire escape. We attended a traditional Navajo dance that was taking place south of the Hubbell Trading Post, about two miles from the campus. On the way one of the boys gave me a nickel to give a dancer if something or other took place. There was a big bonfire going where they were dancing, and I lay down beside it and dozed off.

Someone suddenly woke me up to tell me my shoes were on fire! It was a good thing as they were my only pair of shoes. Sure would have been difficult the following day explaining my burnt shoes, or burnt feet for that matter. We got back safely to the campus and back into the dorm before dawn. I also had to return the nickel I did not use.

On her weekly day off our housemother at the younger boys' dorm usually went to Gallup. We would send our orders with her to purchase "hard to find items" that were not stocked at the local trading post, such as pomade for hair-grooming. Pomade and silk stocking caps went together for the boys' hair-grooming. In the mornings, the users' hair would be plastered to their heads. Not especially flattering. On the other hand, non-use of these grooming

Chapter 7 Boarding School Years

aids resulted in our hair sticking out all over the place, which was not especially flattering either.

We all survived those years and came out looking pretty good by the time we graduated. (I'll brag since nobody ever bragged about us.) At the older boys' dorm, Noxzema was the popular facial care choice as one could smell it all over the place in the mornings. The perfume, Evening in Paris, must have been popular with the girls as one could get a whiff of it at special occasions.

We were required to wear ties to church on Sundays. The first Sunday, Walter did not want to wear his tie, so the housemother had to enlist Daniel's help to deal with him. He was able to talk Walter into putting one on. Wearing a tie was a "first" for Walter and me, and I imagine this was true for most of the new arrivals. Sheep herding did not require us to wear ties. My first tie was tan in color, and it had a picture of a horse's head inside a horseshoe.

Our ties were pretty gravy-stained by the end of the school year, but it didn't seem to bother us. Most of us wore the clip-on ties as we had no previous experience with tying them. However, by the time my class graduated from the 9th grade, the boys knew how to tie bow ties as the girls in our class made bow ties for us.

The girls also made their own dresses to wear for the graduation ceremony. According to one of my classmates, the Home Economics teacher suggested they make their own dresses, all of similar style, so that none of them would "out-do" the others with a nicer dress. Another reason the teacher gave as to why they should make their own dresses was in case one of them could not afford to buy a dress of their own.[16]

After moving to the senior dorm we no longer did some of the things we did in the other dorm; we had "matured". We evidently hadn't though; nor had we gotten much smarter. One night after the lights went out (bed time), my roommates and I decided to pop some popcorn. We had a popper that didn't have a

Right Place, Right Time

lid, so we used an aluminum pie tin. The popcorn popper, which we had set on the floor in the middle of the room, began popping and pinging, making all kinds of racket. I imagine a regular cover would not have made much of a difference anyway, noise-wise.

We were in our beds pretending to be asleep when the room light came on. None of us dared to move as we knew the housefather was standing by the door, probably trying to control himself from pulling us out of bed one at a time. I can't recall what was said, or what the punishment was, other than the fact that we didn't see our popcorn popper again for quite some time.

Never a Dull Moment

Most of the things we did for fun involved playing tricks on each other and on the staff and trying to get away with various shenanigans. We did get into mischief, but most were not serious enough to get us expelled, or to be denied re-admission. The geographical location of the Mission did insulate us from the more serious problems resulting from drugs and alcohol, although not completely.

One night Daniel and one or two other boys and I took (stole is the more appropriate word) bikes belonging to staff members from the front of their living quarters. As we were riding them on campus we suddenly saw car lights approaching us from the rear. We immediately got off the bikes and began running across the unlit yard of the nurses' quarters. Unbeknownst to us there was a clothesline in the yard. I got "clotheslined" literally across my neck and got knocked to the ground. There I was on the ground gasping for air as my own brother and our accomplices went into hiding.

After recovering, I was able to get back in the dorm, probably with a red line across my throat. I don't think my accomplices ever checked on me to see if I was okay. So much for the students looking after each other.

Chapter 7 Boarding School Years

Below the sidewalks on the campus were tunnels that led to all the buildings as they were used for transferring the utilities from the power plant. One night we entered one of these tunnels through a manhole near the high school building and found our way into a section of the school basement that was used for storing supplies. Cases of soft drinks were stored in there, and since we didn't dare turn on any lights, we opened bottles of pop of unknown flavors. We drank a bottle each and didn't take any with us as what we opened were not our preferred drinks.

We went back through the tunnel and out without getting caught even though the campus had a night watchman. Despite the many out-of-dorm escapades that went on, I don't think he ever caught anyone.

During this time period sodas were sold from machines resembling large metal ice chests. Inside the chests, the bottles stood upright, the upper part of the bottles appearing above the metal dividers separating the rows of bottles of different flavors. To purchase a bottle, one inserted a dime, yes! a dime, into a coin slot at one end, thereby allowing the person to pull a bottle out of the chest.

One such machine was located inside the gymnasium. We learned that it was possible to open a pop bottle while it was still standing in the chest, and by using a straw we were able to sip a delicious bottle of soda without having to pay for it.

There was a parlor connecting the chapel and the church. The parlor had nice living-room type-furniture, and a telephone. We would sneak into the parlor at night, relax in the chairs in the dark, and use the telephone to call the girl friends in the dormitory.

One night we were sitting in the parlor when we heard a door open. We jumped up and headed for the back door to escape and ran right into the minister who was entering the building. He evidently did not recognize us as it was dark, but it was a close call.

Right Place, Right Time

One major food heist ended badly. Several of us planned to pull this off during our Saturday morning work detail in the kitchen. The plan was to take the stolen food out with the trash and place it among card board boxes where the trash was placed for pick up by "Grandpa Shondee", an elderly Navajo man who collected the trash and hauled it off to the dump in his horse-drawn wagon.

He picked it up at a certain time on Saturdays, usually after lunch, and we were going collect the booty before he did. I don't know what happened. Either he came early, or we were late getting to the trash collection site, which was behind the kitchen. By the time we got there the trash was gone, and so was our food!

One of the major items we had hidden among the card board boxes were eggs which we had planned to take to the nearby lake to fix that afternoon. We must have planned to boil them as we didn't have any oil or pan to cook them in. Anyway, our great plan blew up on us.

Extra-Curricular Activities

Friday nights were free. We had movies that were shown in the gym every other Friday night. The movies were selected by a committee made up of students and faculty; of course the faculty member(s) held the veto power on film selection. So, we never saw any racy movies, just films like *Bambi* and *The Living Desert*. I'm joking, barely. We saw "action films" like *Zorro*, and the following day the younger boys would be wearing capes and fighting with swords they made from cardboard.

The movies came on three large reels and the school principal was the projectionist. The reel changes were hated as there was a lull in the movie and the lights came on, interrupting whatever else was taking place in the audience. It cost us a dime to get in.

Chapter 7 Boarding School Years

Movie nights and athletic events gave the student organizations, and especially the senior class, opportunities to make money by selling popcorn. The seniors needed the money to finance their senior trip at the end of the year. My class of 1958 went on a camping trip to Oak Creek Canyon near Flagstaff, Arizona, which was a lot of fun.

There were two major student productions each year. One was the senior class play that took place in the spring. My class play had a South Pacific theme, and I played the role of a butler. I've never forgotten one of my lines in the play, "I'm all agog myself, sir". I don't think I ever knew what the word agog meant.

The second production was the Christmas Pageant put on by the students and faculty. It was really quite impressive, and it was a major event for the parents, people from the surrounding area, and the mission personnel and students.

We were always anxious to get out of the dorm in the evenings so we generally didn't mind the evening study halls. Just to get out of the dorm, I joined the school band and tried to learn to play the trombone, most times having to pretend that I was actually blowing the horn. I may have been asked to leave the band when my trombone began sounding like it wasn't supposed to sound. Or, I blew it at the wrong place in the piece we were playing.

We were given about twenty minutes to get back to the dormitories after our evening activities. This barely gave us enough time to walk the girlfriends back to their dorms, then to our own dorms.

There were other extracurricular activities that went on during the week, not leaving a whole of time to be idle. There were organizational meetings and combined social activities. While dancing was not allowed, the girls still tried to teach us guys to dance even on chaperoned outings. Once we were at Canyon de Chelly for an outing, and the girls tried to teach us to dance. Can you imagine

Right Place, Right Time

trying to learn how to dance on the sandstone rim of the Canyon? No wonder I never learned.

There was a small lake within walking distance of the campus where the boys could walk to fish on weekends. Our fishing equipment consisted of long sticks for fishing poles and twine. I don't remember if we ever caught any fish.

The Mission personnel also fielded a basketball team, competing with teams from the surrounding area. The boys living in the senior dorm were sometimes allowed to attend their home games, even keeping score for them. I was the score keeper for one of their games, which was very close. With only a few seconds left in the game, with the Mission team ahead maybe by one point, they called a time-out. When the time-out was over, I forgot to turn the clock back on, and the opposing team scored and won the game.

You can imagine how angry the team was with me, and one of the members really chewed me out. I happened to run into him many years later. I asked him if he remembered the incident. He didn't. I kidded him by telling him that I didn't know that missionaries were allowed to use the type of language he used chewing me out. He really didn't use any derogatory language, honest. He got a good laugh out of this reminder.

Interpersonal Relationships

A characteristic I have always cherished about my Ganado Mission experience was the sense of closeness among the students. I sensed this almost immediately upon my arrival at the Mission. The students were really good to each other. Many of the older students took the younger ones under their wings. Rather than pushing off the younger ones, or taking advantage of them, these older students were protective of us. The exception may have been my own brother who didn't even bother to check on me after I was downed by the clothesline during our bike-stealing escapade.

Chapter 7 Boarding School Years

I had this special kind of relationship with a Hopi student who was a junior when I got to Ganado. What strikes me as being really unique was that years later I reread his girlfriend's autograph. She wrote that Emerson, my friend, would still be at Ganado when I returned for my eighth grade year. She was reassuring me that I would still have him to look after me. Too, can you imagine a high school senior autographing a seventh grader's year book today?

We shared what little most of us had, especially the food we got from home. I don't know why we always seemed to eat after the lights went out at bedtime. We would sit in the dark eating. Mother would occasionally send us a box of food like oven bread, cooked mutton ribs, and other foods we ate at home. At the beginning of school we brought back some of these foods, including such produce as watermelons, etc. Upon returning to school one time, Evelyn was too embarrassed to carry her watermelon from the truck to her dorm. She made Daniel take it to her front door.

I especially enjoyed the parched corn and piki, paper bread, the Hopi students brought back with them or received from home. When I occupied one of the two-student rooms in my 9th grade year, my roommate and I hung our box of food outside our north facing second floor window with a rope, hoping the perishable food would last longer in the shade.

Virgil was one of my roommates after I moved to the Senior Dormitory. Virgil was a grade ahead of me and was also from Guishsche. One time his parents came to visit him, and they brought him some fried chicken. That evening he shared this with us, his roommates. As we were devouring the chicken, Virgil told us that it was pheasant we were eating. I actually believed him. After we wolfed down the "pheasant", he confessed that it was chicken. It wasn't Kentucky Fried Chicken either, as the franchise was only a few years old. Virgil's mother, one of the kindest persons I know, worked at the local day school when the Carrs were going through there.

Right Place, Right Time

There was a lot of teasing that went on among the students, some of which could be considered mean-spirited. Yes, there were a few bullies. Nothing compared to the numbers that now seem to be in the schools today. I can't really recall any actual fisticuffs ever breaking out. There was name calling which I experienced, and branding of individuals, including the staff, with nicknames which may not have always been complimentary.

Practically everyone had a nickname. I didn't think I ever had one, but my classmate, Marilyn, nicknamed Sammie, referred to me as "Dusty" in a PowerPoint presentation she prepared for our class of 1958 reunion. Nicknames resulted from a variety of ways, some of which I'm scared to cite. Nicknames such as Nazlini Hill, Rooster, Statue, and Juke Box are a few examples.

Classes also had nicknames. My class was called the Gophers. I don't know how the name originated. The class behind us was called Wild Horses, and the class behind them was the Frogs. I do remember the origin of Wild Horses. This class could be heard coming down the hallway from afar, thundering like a herd of wild horses.

There were a number of schoolmates whom I considered to be close friends. However, I tend to think that interrelationships within groups overshadowed, to some degree the one-to-one relationships. Of course the dating relationships were the exception. We lived together in dormitories, ate all our meals together, and attended classes together, etc. So our living situation impacted our interrelationships.

Sure, there were schoolmates whose company I enjoyed more than others and some who were more special than others. However, it is the friendliness of the student body and Mission personnel that I have always cherished.

Chapter 7 Boarding School Years

Athletics

Athletics were popular, and there were many good athletes, both boys and girls. We had the full slate of competitive sports, and the teams competed with schools located in northeastern Arizona and western New Mexico. We also competed against Menaul School in Albuquerque. We had intramural competition that provided opportunities for all the students who wanted to participate in athletics.

There was a vacant lot between the high school building and dining hall that we used for gym classes. This is where we also played 'work up" softball games after supper in which both boys and girls played.

We had a tennis court that was used mainly by the Mission personnel and their children. Evidently the game of tennis had yet to reach the reservations. There was also an outdoor swimming pool that was open only during the summer months. Students who remained there for the summer were able to use it. Soccer may have already been a sport played in the cities, but I don't recall it being played during the time I was at Ganado.

Women's basketball was played under different rules than it is today. The offense played on half the court, and the defense played the other half. There were six players to a team, three playing offense, and the other three playing defense. There were quite a few very talented female basketball players, especially from my class. Gym classes and our pickup softball games were a lot of fun. One student who would never swing at a pitch quickly earned the nickname of "Statue".

There were other organized group activities. One event that I recall was "Talent Night". The students organized activities to display their talents to the student body. One of the older boys organized a team of elementary grade students, my brother Walter being one of them, as the Harlem Globetrotters. They did a few

Right Place, Right Time

dribbling tricks and mimicked other tricks the Globetrotters performed. Another event was an indoor intramural track meet.

They may not have been ongoing events, but these stand out as staff efforts to encourage students to organize and participate in group activities. Outside of Saturday and Sunday mornings which were reserved for work, church, and Sunday school, the remainder of the weekend was our free time.

During the football, basketball, and baseball seasons we had both home and away games. Away games for football and basketball that were close to our school, allowed some of the students to attend. It was rugged riding the bus to the schools located on or to the south of U. S. Route 66, now I-40. We had to travel thirty eight miles on the unpaved washboard road between Ganado and Route 66. Before I graduated a used "Greyhound-like" bus with reclining seats was donated to the Mission, and we were able to travel more comfortably. The away games were a lot of fun. When we won, there was a lot of singing on the way home. The coach was also the bus driver.

1956 Ganado Panthers. 9-1 Record. I'm No. 36.

Chapter 7 Boarding School Years

In my junior year we lost only one football game, to Gallup High School, which was a much bigger school. The Oklahoma Sooners, coached by Bud Wilkinson, who were in the midst of a forty seven game winning streak, served as our model, copying their style of play.

In 1957 their 47 game winning streak was broken by Notre Dame, the same day we lost a game. I remember commenting on the Sooners' loss to the coach as we were coming off the field. His reaction told me that was not the most appropriate time, or subject, to raise right after our own loss.

I had no idea at the time that I would actually be sitting in the stands watching the Sooners play Oklahoma State the following fall in Stillwater, Oklahoma. During our Thanksgiving break I attended the game with my college friend, Ted, and his friends who were students at Oklahoma State.

1957 Ganado Panthers' Backfield. Me at Quarterback

I was never an outstanding athlete. I did play baseball as a 2nd baseman and quarterback in football during my last three years

Right Place, Right Time

of high school. I played basketball in junior high and was trying out for the varsity basketball team when I had an opportunity to go to Phoenix to attend a Westminster Fellowship function. Westminster Fellowship is the Presbyterian Church's young people's organization. My primary motivation for wanting to go to Phoenix however was a chance to see my girlfriend who was a student at the Phoenix Indian School.

The coach told me I had to make a choice between basketball and attending the function in Phoenix. I didn't tell him about the girl friend. If he knew, he would have probably banned me from all his teams permanently. I'm kidding. My choice of the trip ended my potential basketball career. It's doubtful that I would have made the team anyway as there were many good players, and I was not the most talented basketball player.

Three of the football team's quarterbacks between about 1955-1957 were from Guishsche. They were my brother, Daniel, Virgil, the guy who served me "pheasant", and me. Both Daniel and Virgil were very good Single Wing quarterbacks, the football formation that was played at the time. We later switched to the T-formation before I graduated. Although I played first string my final year, I wasn't at Dan's and Virgil's level.

Just as dad's uncle, Frank Hudson, had excelled in drop-kicking at Carlisle, Daniel was a very good drop-kicker. This was the technique that was used for kicking field goals through about the mid 1950's. The kicker dropped the football in front of him, and it had to touch the ground before it could be kicked for an attempted field goal. I believe this took more skill than the current way of kicking them. Daniel tells of how he practiced so hard for one particular game that by the time the actual game was played his kicking leg "was gone".

I must complement the school's coaching staff of one. The personnel on our sidelines were not equally divided between the

Chapter 7 Boarding School Years

athletes and coaches, or at least it looks that way today. Only one person coached all the teams, taught Physical Education, lined the football field, and drove the team bus. The science teacher was the lone volunteer assistant coach. This is especially impressive as the coaches who were there at different times during my six years really fielded good teams in every sport played at the school.

I Actually Attended Classes

I don't want to give you the impression that my six years at Ganado were just fun and games. Honestly, I did actually go to school five days a week during my six years.

Dorm Mates Studying

I learned a lot in the classroom, enjoyed most of my classes and had very devoted teachers who tried hard to teach me. As an accredited high school all the teachers had degrees in their teaching areas. We had all the basic and typical courses taught in public schools. The only ones that may have differed were probably the required religious education classes.

We had a few elective courses from which to choose. The only one I can recall is the typing class. We learned to type on manual typewriters, and this class turned out to be extremely valuable in graduate school. I didn't have access to a typewriter during my first four years of college. My high school years were way

Right Place, Right Time

before electric typewriters and computers, and I should mention, satellite television. We didn't even have television at the Mission, and evidently its absence did not cause us any lasting damage.

Based on my experience during my freshman year in college, I'd have to say that the curriculum content must have been pretty basic, particularly in math and the sciences. I found my schoolmates to be far more advanced in these areas than me. My brother, Daniel, who became a civil engineer, said that he learned the most from his post high school math and science courses.

Some of the instruction was stronger than others, and I must have learned a lot from my English classes as I left there with good writing skills. Despite some weaknesses in the curriculum content, most of us who went on to various areas of higher education were able to complete our coursework successfully.

As opposed to the focus on vocational training in the government boarding schools, our school was geared more to academics. Our daily work details gave us work experience. The school also provided us with many other opportunities that prepared us for independent living.

I learned how to wash and iron my own clothes, and in my senior year there was a required home economics class for the boys. In this class I learned how to maneuver the spoon eating soup, how to set the table, and how to seat the girls at the table. This really came in handy at Emporia as we had one weekly dinner that was more "formal" than other meals.

The most fun was the biscuit-making. As we were mixing the ingredients, every time this one student turned his head, we would toss in his mixing bowl additional ingredients. When the biscuits came out of the oven, his biscuits were hard as rock. He never figured why his turned out that way.

The Home Economics department was housed in a separate building resembling a private residence. In fact, the Home

Chapter 7 Boarding School Years

Economics teacher lived there, and in their senior year the girls took turns living there to provide them with independent living experience.

It was only after I graduated that I appreciated the importance of what the school tried to teach us about independent living. At home I would never have learned how to wash my own clothes, much less learn how to iron them. By the way, we even ironed jeans during my day. All these experiences came in handy after I left.

The teachers were very much committed to our learning, and they were dedicated to providing us sound instruction. I don't know how well they were paid, nor do I know what resources they had to work with. I do know that they recognized whatever potential we had and tried to nurture that potential. I never felt that there was a teacher or Mission employee who was there just biding their time. These were dedicated people. The campus was isolated. The closest town of Gallup was fifty three miles away. Too, we as students may not have been the easiest to teach as we were from varied backgrounds and tribes. None of our teachers at the time were Indian.

I had several favorite teachers and ones I dreaded. The ones whose classes I didn't particularly like, guess what, I have to admit I learned the most from them. One was the English teacher who came after I got there. My other favorite teachers and classes were math and religious education. I later found out that I didn't learn math that well. The Religious Education teacher and the minister probably had the most influence on me through my participation in Westminster Fellowship. However, I learned something from all my teachers.

I dreaded the art classes. Most of the students were very artistic, and I have to assume that we had a good teacher. I've never had any artistic talent, other than using shoe polish to paint

Right Place, Right Time

mustaches, beards, etc., on the faces of sleeping dorm-mates. These classes were difficult for me. However, it was in the art class during my senior year that I had an opportunity to learn the basics of drafting. I actually learned how to draw, using a ruler. This experience led me to want to become a mechanical engineer, which I never became.

The late renowned artist, R. C. Gorman, is one example of a most talented artist who went to school at Ganado. There are other students who have produced prize-winning art and have provided leadership in the world of art.

Speaking of the late Mr. Gorman, he was Kathryn's school mate. She happened to run into him at the New Mexico State Fair after he became famous. Before parting, he reached into his satchel and gave her several of his original drawings. Remember what I said earlier about how the students were so good to each other. This is a good example of the long-lasting relationships we developed as students, as well as remaining close to the school which is now closed. Well-attended reunions of the students and staff continue to this day, reliving our fun days through often repeated stories.

We had a Student Council made up of two representatives from each class. I served on the Council several times and served as its president in my senior year. Daniel and Evelyn also served in various capacities on the Council, but they can't remember what positions they held. I gained much of my leadership experience and self-confidence from serving on the student council and in several Westminster Fellowship positions.

I earned a number of scholastic awards during my final three years, including getting on the Honor Roll several times. I was recognized as the top science student in my senior year. While these recognitions did a lot for my self-confidence, I did very poorly in my college math and science courses.

Chapter 7 Boarding School Years

The Carr children all gained reputations as being "smart". Of course it was nice to hear, but I've always thought that persistence and never giving up would be more descriptive of us.

All these experiences established a foundation for my eventual "successes" in my educational and other life pursuits. I don't know how I would have fared in a large public school setting, especially where Indian students were in the minority. This small and caring church-oriented boarding school definitely served as a near perfect setting for me in my transition from my close-knit, church-going, sheep-herding family to my years after high school.

Westminster Fellowship

The other major segment of my high school experience was my religious education. Since church attendance was a part of the Carr children's upbringing, the school's religious education requirements were a natural extension of my life at home. I don't know who influenced our parents to send us to Ganado rather than to a government boarding school. My parents were evidently convinced that Ganado Mission would fulfill their two most important aspirations for their children, which was a religious upbringing and the attainment of an education. I was too young to recognize that these were our parents' aspirations for us at the time. However looking back at how we had to attend church and school leaves little doubt about what they wanted for us.

It was this background that I brought with me as a twelve year old. I felt very comfortable with the school's requirements, such as attending Sunday school, church services, the weekly chapel services, and taking religious education classes. Soon after I arrived, I became involved in Westminster Fellowship.

My participation eventually led to numerous opportunities would not have experienced had I attended a government boarding school, and for sure, if I had remained at home. I got involved in

Right Place, Right Time

planning, organizing, and leading meetings; speaking before groups; and leading chapel services. I got to attend meetings and summer camps that involved other young people from various churches throughout Arizona.

On one of these trips to southern Arizona, we visited the state prison in Florence. I think the chaperones wanted to show us where we would end up if we didn't behave. I'm kidding.

I also took two major trips while at Ganado. The first one was a five week cross-country trip to New York and back with seven school mates and three chaperones in the summer of 1956, between my sophomore and junior years. Each of us had to earn $75.00 for personal spending, which we earned doing odd jobs for the mission staff. One of the teachers gave each of us a $2.00 bill on the day we left, which was right after school ended in May.

We traveled in two vehicles. We may have driven only as far as Baltimore and left the vehicles with relatives of one of the chaperones. We must have taken a train to New York City and back to Baltimore as I don't remember driving into New York City. We spoke before church congregations and spent nights with church families. After leaving Ganado, our first day's lunch stop was at the Presbyterian Church manse at Laguna. There I found three new pairs of socks my brother, Daniel, had left for me.

Chapter 7 Boarding School Years

This trip put into use the experiences I had gained from speaking before groups. After our selection for this trip, we began traveling to different churches to speak before congregations. One of the places we spoke was at the Laguna Presbyterian Church at Casa Blanca. My mother was in attendance, but we never talked about my "sermon." I'm sure she was proud of me. My involvement in Westminster Fellowship probably reassured her that I was at least on the path that she envisioned for her children, that is putting into practice what she taught us about her religious faith.

On the way east we spoke in several Black churches in Mississippi and Virginia. We also visited several Black colleges. As their guests we stayed in two Black hotels in West Point, Mississippi and Roanoke, Virginia. What I knew about the discrimination against Blacks was from newspapers and what I saw on the news reels that were shown in one of my classes. That these two churches could not book us into any hotel introduced me to how they were treated.

At the time I was too naïve to understand the full implications of that experience as this was completely new to me. Growing up on a reservation and then attending a boarding school that was also located on a reservation had shielded me from racial discrimination. During my six years at Ganado, we had only two Black school mates who were brothers, and two teachers who were Black.

Experiences involving racial discrimination would come after leaving Ganado for many of us. Most of my brothers and sisters experienced it. Five of my female classmates who were entering nurse's training in Dallas, Texas in 1958 were traveling together by bus to their new school. At the Amarillo, Texas bus depot they were confronted with having to ask which of two bathrooms to use, the one designated for "Whites" or the one for "Colored". Not knowing which one to use, they asked. They were asked what race they were. They told the agent they were American Indians, and she told them

117

Right Place, Right Time

to use the one for "Whites".[17] Daniel also experienced the separate bathroom scenario in Virginia Beach, Virginia where he was stationed at a naval base.

This trip was filled with new experiences for all of us. Other than the summer I spent in Oklahoma with my family, I had never been out of the states of New Mexico and Arizona. As far as I know, neither had my fellow student travelers. I saw first-hand what I had only seen from pictures in magazines or read about.

For example, we visited the Oak Ridge National Laboratory in Tennessee as well as one of the dams in the Tennessee Valley Authority (TVA) system. In New York City we visited the United Nations. Dag Hammarskjold was the Secretary-General of the United Nations at the time.

Here I was in the summer of 1956 sitting in the gallery inside this world organization's building using earphones listening to a speech being translated into English. Hard to believe as I was still herding sheep the previous summer. Never in my wildest dreams did I see myself being a tourist in one of the world's largest cities this particular summer.

We went to a baseball game in Yankee Stadium and visited many of the tourist sites in New York City. We even attended a Broadway show, *Pajama Game*. At the Empire State Building we met a guard who was a fellow Indian from the state of Oregon.

We appeared on a local TV show. I hope I remember correctly the details of our curious experience. The show would not allow the late Ferrell Secakuku, who later became the Chairman of his Hopi Tribe, to use a drum to sing a Hopi song due to a union-related issue. That didn't stop Ferrell. He used, I believe, a cardboard box as his drum and shared a bit of his culture with the show's TV audience. Several of the students dressed in their native clothes at some of our appearances, including the TV show. The eight of us represented the Hopi, Laguna, and Navajo tribes.

Chapter 7 Boarding School Years

In Baltimore we saw the movie, *The Man Who Knew Too Much*, which had as its theme song, *Que Sera Sera, Whatever Will Be, Will Be*. We had to listen to our late schoolmate, Juke Box, sing this song for us all the way back to New Mexico. Yes, she was named Juke Box because of her constant singing. I used a portion of the $75.00 I had earned for this trip to purchase a wristwatch, a Waltham, in Baltimore.

In Washington D. C. we visited our Nation's Capital and all the various monuments, including a visit to Congress. I can't quite remember whether it was on this visit to Washington, that we visited Senator Barry Goldwater in his Senate office, or whether we visited him at his home in Phoenix. I do remember that we had a personal visit with him, and I especially remember all the Native craft work displayed in his office, or home. Senator Goldwater always made our school one of his political campaign stops as I remember him speaking from our band stand.

We were also special guests of the New York Avenue Church in Washington. Our group was seated in the President Abraham Lincoln pew. He had attended this church during his presidency. I didn't know at the time that President Lincoln had presented canes to each of the Pueblo governors in 1865 to signify the government's recognition of the Pueblos' tribal governments. Today the engraved cane serves as a symbol of the Office of our tribal Governor.

My second major trip was to the Westminster Fellowship National Assembly of High School Students at Grinnell College in Iowa in 1957. I went with one of my school mates and with other young people from the Phoenix and Tucson areas. We traveled together by bus. It was during this trip that I became friends with a guy from southern Arizona who later starred as a quarterback for the University of Arizona Wildcats, and then played professional football in the American Football League.

Right Place, Right Time

I was ostracized by a few of my schoolmates for my involvement in Westminster Fellowship. I was quite active in this organization, but I don't think I ever made a spectacle of myself. My mother often told us that we may be ridiculed at times for what we stand for, but it must not deter us from doing what is right. My problem was my parents were not present to provide immediate support, and I didn't feel comfortable discussing it with the Mission personnel.

Luckily, just about the time I was going through this experience, the Reverend Roe B. Lewis came to our school to spend a week as the guest minister for the school's Spiritual Emphasis Week. The Reverend Lewis, a Pima-Papago Indian, is a graduate of the San Francisco Theological Seminary and was later awarded an honorary Doctor of Divinity degree from Dubuque University. I later learned that the Reverend Lewis was the first ordained Indian minister in the United Presbyterian Church who had a complete college and theological education.[18]

The Reverend Lewis held worship services for the students and staff and provided religious counseling during this particular week. I became very impressed with him because he was an Indian, and he was a trained minister. I gained a great deal of support from him about my role in Westminster Fellowship, and what he had to say about Christianity impressed me.

My Westminster Fellowship participation and the experiences I gained from it rounded out my boarding school experience. I am forever grateful that somebody convinced my parents to send me to Ganado Mission. It was here that the missionaries helped me to integrate their teachings with what I learned from my parents and the people of my village which would forever guide me.

Chapter 7 Boarding School Years

Planning for College, Spring 1958

I imagine as a result of all my experiences, I knew by my senior year that I wanted to go to college. Mechanical engineering interested me as the result of my class in drafting. I had gotten good grades in all my classes, including my math and science courses.

In early spring I began looking through a handbook of Presbyterian-related schools. One school in Pennsylvania got my attention. The catalog showed a picture of a student in a military-looking uniform. I thought I would look pretty good in such a uniform, and I briefly considered applying there. This association involving the uniform must have been based on my early experiences of seeing soldiers returning home in their military uniforms and how sharp they looked, including my brother Elgin. I think the school's high tuition helped change my mind.

I don't think I ever thought about the distances these schools were from either Ganado or from home. I must have been pretty self-confident already, thinking I could succeed wherever I went, or more likely, pretty naive.

It's interesting to me now that I never considered any of the state colleges in either New Mexico or Arizona. I knew next to nothing about the University of New Mexico, located just fifty five miles from Guishsche and in the midst of twenty two reservations. I don't know how much of an effort, if any, this university, or for that matter, any university, made in recruiting Indian students at the time. I do know Indians became quite popular after federal monies became available in the 1960's, and many universities suddenly became interested in Indian students. It was during this period that many "Indian Studies" programs sprouted up.

I eventually settled on the College of Emporia in Kansas. I may have selected Emporia because my brother, Daniel, had gone there for his freshmen year in 1956, and he may have encouraged me to enroll there. There were several other recent Ganado

Right Place, Right Time

graduates who had gone to Emporia. By the time I got there, two of them, who were Evelyn's classmates, had already graduated, and the others were also gone.

With the help of a faculty member, I applied for and received a scholarship from the Board of National Missions of the Presbyterian Church. I may have also received one from Emporia as my tuition, room and board, and books were covered. I graduated from Ganado Mission High School in May, 1958, along with eighteen classmates.

Class of 1958--I'm in the back row, second from left.

In three months I would begin the next major segment of my journey. I had developed enough self-confidence by then that I looked forward to taking this next step. My family and the Mission faculty had done their best to prepare me, and I've never been disappointed by their efforts on my behalf.

Chapter 7 Boarding School Years

Leaving Ganado

I left Ganado for the last time right after the conclusion of our graduation ceremonies. As I left my thoughts were focused primarily on the fact that I was leaving behind all my friends. I didn't know if I would see them again.

50th Reunion, Class of 1958

In addition, I had grown to love the place where I had lived for parts of six years and where I had enjoyed so many different experiences and friendships. As one of my sisters put it, Ganado had become "our home". Only years later did I begin to think about the pluses and minuses of my boarding school experiences. As a result I gained a greater appreciation of the impact this school had on me.

The Mission faculty and staff did a most credible job of helping me develop the tools for dealing with life after graduation. However, I believe no matter how good a boarding school may be, it minimizes the role of parents.

Right Place, Right Time

My parents had little involvement in discussions and decisions regarding my future, such as helping me decide whether to go to work, whether to attend a vocational school, or whether to attend college after I finished high school. We did not talk about where the money was going to come from to pay for additional schooling. Even though we went home during the summer months and for the Christmas holidays, we never got around to discussing these major decisions, or we just shied away from discussing them because we didn't know how to talk about them.

I and my siblings made these big decisions while we were still teenagers with the guidance coming from the school personnel, rather than our parents. However, what I learned from my parents was enough to guide me as I planned with the faculty for my continued schooling.

Attending boarding school also minimized the opportunities of learning how to share my thoughts, ideas, and feelings within my family. Even though Evelyn, Daniel, Walter, and I were at Ganado at the same time, we rarely took time to just be together. If we did talk, it was only in passing. Each of us was more focused on our individual activities, and what went on in our immediate surroundings, like the dorms and classrooms.

About the only times we spent together were on school breaks. Even then, we rarely had any serious discussions with each other. Despite how good Ganado was, boarding schools in general are not able to provide some of the important experiences we learn from growing up within a family setting.

Just as important was the absence of my parents when personal issues arose, especially those I did not feel comfortable in sharing with the staff. Just the sharing of every day experiences with parents was absent. I didn't realize it at the time, but children growing up in boarding schools are deprived of many of the familial relationships that enhance personal growth and development.

Chapter 7 Boarding School Years

My houseparent in the junior dorm was a very kind lady. She would turn on the lights each morning with, "it's time to get up now, boys." My parents would give me the same command to get out of bed, Tro o ipiti, Sah mudi, Get out of bed, my son. While the commands are similar, somehow it's different when your own parent gives you this command. However, I give full credit to the school for helping me meet my parents' aspirations for me and for starting me on an adventurous journey.

Finally, there are two major areas of my personal growth where Ganado had the greatest impact. The first area has to do with the fact that the school served as a bridge for my transition from life on the reservation to later life in college and beyond. The school strengthened and further developed what I learned from my family and my fellow villagers. It provided me a protective and supportive environment in which I was given the leeway to experiment as a way to learn and to grow.

In addition, the faculty recognized and acknowledged the strengths I had shown, and they nurtured these strengths. The Mission personnel, both staff and teachers provided me opportunities to develop the strengths they must have seen in me, such as my classroom work, my Westminster Fellowship roles, and other roles that I played as a student. The school also expanded my horizons through my travels and my involvement with students from other schools.

The stories I've shared about my school experiences involving the relationships among students and faculty are examples of how Ganado Mission made it fun to be educated there. If I had to identify a period of my life which was one of the happiest, without a doubt, my days at this school would be close to the top.

Right Place, Right Time

Home All Together, A Rarity for the Carr Family

Having to attend boarding school created the separations experienced by our family. As each of us reached the age of ten or twelve, we left home. About every other year, beginning in about 1939 until 1952, a Carr sibling left home for Ganado Mission. This migration began with our oldest sister, Kathryn. Walter and I were the last to leave home. According to a paper Kathryn later wrote for one of her classes, she was "really lonesome for about four months". She said she cried, but she "couldn't help it". She also wrote that she always wanted "to thank my parents for sending me off to this school which I love dearly ---"

Once we got into boarding school, all of us began working at various jobs and locations during the summer. Some of us stayed and worked at the Mission for our tuition. Evelyn baby sat for a family in Albuquerque, and another summer she took a Mission-sponsored trip to Chicago and back with several students, just like I did in 1956. I stayed one summer, and two summers I took the trips to New York and Grinnell, Iowa. If we were not working, we were at the sheep camp herding sheep, certainly an incentive to work elsewhere.

How did we get these jobs? Kathryn said it was the Reverend James Ottipoby, a Comanche who was the Presbyterian minister at Laguna the latter part of the 1940's who lined up many of the summer jobs for the Carr children. We lined up a few jobs ourselves, like staying at the Mission. Kathryn said she began staying there after her eighth grade year, earning $35.00 a month, $25.00 going toward her year's tuition. Several of my older siblings spent summers with relatives in Barstow. One summer Evelyn worked on a special project with other college students building a water storage tank for the Mission.

Both work and school affected the amount of time the family was together. The Christmas holidays were the times many of us did

Chapter 7 Boarding School Years

return home. I later learned that it was not until 1973 that all of us were home at the same time due to our family's tragic loss of Edna and her husband, Francis, as a result of a car accident caused by a drunken driver.

Me, Evelyn, Walter, Daniel

The Christmas holidays when we were able to get home, we did fun things together. For example, one year several of us went caroling with some cousins. Some dogs chased us as we were caroling up in the northwest part of the village. There was about a foot of snow on the ground, and I remember all of us ran in different directions. We kept falling as it was hard running in the deep snow.

Many years later, a woman in front of whose home we sang, told Kathryn that her husband had referred to us as "those Angels!" I have always remembered this as it was the first and only time I've been referred to as an angel. Her husband, Tony, was a favorite relative. He always addressed us boys as "Brother." His father and my paternal grandfather were related.

We built our own sleds, one large enough for several of us to ride on together. One evening several of us, along with friends, went

Right Place, Right Time

sledding on the road going north out of the village. We were sledding on this fairly steep incline, where at the bottom the road veered sharply to the left. As we were sledding, we heard a truck coming out of the village that sounded like it was going at a high rate of speed. We quickly got off the road. Sure enough, a pickup truck appeared at the top of the hill and sped down the slippery road. It didn't negotiate the left turn, and the truck turned over on its side right in front of us. We immediately ran down to the truck. As we got there, the driver, who was drunk, was crawling out the window.

Luckily, he had not gotten hurt. The truck may not have turned completely over on its side as we were able to help him right the truck and he got back in and drove off as if nothing happened. We finished sledding and couldn't wait to get home to tell our parents about this experience.

Another thing we did together during the Christmas holidays was attend the Christmas Eve Indian dances, which took place in the Catholic Church. I don't recall my parents ever attending. After the dances were over, which would be after one o'clock in the morning, we came home, and mom and dad would be waiting for us with food on the table.[19] The food was generally venison jerky, along with other foods that we ate at home.

We'd sit around the table eating and laughing, just having a great time as a family. We didn't exchange Christmas gifts, nor did we have a Christmas tree, yet these were the Christmas celebrations I'll always cherish.

On these rare occasions when we were together our parents talked to us about their expectations of us, and reminded us of how we should treat each other. One of their often repeated reminders was that if we had differences among us that we resolve them in a responsible way and not remain angry at each other. We have never carried this out to perfection, but on the whole we as adults have tried hard to honor this one particular parental expectation.

Chapter 7 Boarding School Years

They always acknowledged in their own way how well we all seemed to be doing, whether it was about school or work. I don't recall ever hearing the phrase, "we are proud of you." They always told us how thankful they were about how we were living our lives, which seemed to be their way of telling us they were proud.

After Evelyn became an elementary school teacher she took them to the Pueblo of Isleta Day School where she was teaching to show them her classroom. She could tell how proud they were of her. After we began working, Daniel and I arranged for them to come visit us. Daniel was working in Omaha, and I was in Minneapolis. So when they were around the age of sixty, mom and dad took their first plane ride.

They spoke to us about how we should act out in public, to obey and to be respectful of others. In addition to wishing us well when we departed from home, there was always this additional counsel without fail: Tramee weh en tkak we yah tru sah, which meant for us to walk with good behavior. I tend to think that was said more to the boys than the girls. This advice continued even after we reached adulthood and until they left us. This pattern of advising children was very typical during this time.

Another regular reminder was to attend church. Mother, particularly, had tremendous faith in God. She would always remind us that he was the source of our strength and that he made all things possible. Do for others and don't worry about what you don't have as our needs will always be met. They backed up all this advice by living it and by the way they raised us.

At the end of the holiday we returned to school riding in the back of our truck, even in winter time. The cabs of pick-up trucks in those days could only accommodate three individuals, and only those with a higher standing in life were able to sit inside. The rest of us had to sit in the back of the truck. Our dad placed a mattress, or pelts, in the truck bed to cushion the ride, and then piled quilts and a

Right Place, Right Time

tarp to cover us on the ride back to school. We never got frostbitten, but those one hundred and fifty mile winter rides in the back of the truck were cold.

Thinking back now, our visits home were merely stops on the way to various destinations such as to schools or places of employment. Home, however, remained as the place we "recharged" ourselves. This had become a way of life for the Carr family, beginning with Kathryn's departure for Ganado in 1939. I don't think staying at Ganado during school breaks was necessarily encouraged by our parents, but because we all liked living there, we volunteered to stay. I even stayed there during one Christmas holiday. One of the reasons I liked to stay was because of the leisure time activities and being with friends. Maybe it also had to do with sheepherding?

Later, when I came home before leaving for college, I was following a pattern that had long been established by the older children. Go home first before heading elsewhere. Mother also insisted that we visit our relatives when we got home, or when we were leaving. I came to appreciate this practice as playing a real important part in the perpetuation of my tribe's and my family's values and customs. The close interrelationships with the extended family formed the base of support for all of us.

While our interrelationships were interrupted by these early separations, we have remained a close knit family. More than any other advice our parents gave us was to love one another and to love one's self, Amu nomasaa kudrus. It was this advice that became a constant reminder, I believe, for each of us. This piece of advice established the foundation for the lasting bond among the Carr children. Even though we separated early, all my brothers and sisters played supportive roles for each other. For me, their support was critical as I struggled to make my way through college.

Chapter 8
Summer, 1958

Upon my graduation in May, Kathryn invited me to spend the summer with her family in Roswell, New Mexico so that I could try to find a summer job. Her husband, a career Airman with the U. S. Air Force, was stationed at Walker Air Force Base in Roswell at the time. I accepted her invitation as I did not have a job lined up for that summer. I got one right away at a Safeway Store about a mile from my sister's house, bagging and carrying out groceries for the customers.

On Saturday evenings the farm workers from the fields around Roswell would come into the store to shop for their groceries. Many of the Hispanic customers thought I was Hispanic and spoke to me in Spanish. When I told them I did not speak Spanish, a few of them got upset with me, thinking I was a Hispanic who did not want to identify with them. This was a new experience for me, not knowing then that I would later be confronted with acts of discrimination based simply on the color of my skin. I enjoyed working at Safeway with the personnel as they were pretty accepting of me.

I became good friends with one of the carryout guys who had also just graduated from high school like me. He had a car that resembled a huge black beetle that transported us to different places and activities. He and I did quite a bit together that summer. We drove over to the Bottomless Lakes State park near Roswell to go swimming. We went out in the desert to shoot his 22 rifle and went to movies at the local Drive-In theatre. I really enjoyed my summer. This was really my first long-term experience working and associating with others who were not of Indian descent. I was now living in a "city" that offered various new opportunities which I had not had

Right Place, Right Time

before. That summer's experience helped me in my transition to college life where none of my school mates would be Indian.

The summer with my sister gave me my first real opportunity to get to know her. This may sound strange to talk about just getting to know my own sister at the age of eighteen. By the time I was born she was already at Ganado. When she graduated from there in 1945, I was only five years old, and she would leave again to attend Biola College in Los Angeles.

After returning home from Biola she began working in Albuquerque, and so we never really lived together. Our relationship had been pretty much limited to her periodic visits home. I do remember a puppet she brought home from Biola named Wally. She also sent me a photo album from Fairbanks, Alaska, where her family was stationed.

The summer in Roswell, therefore, gave us the first real opportunity in getting to know each other. I remember this particular summer as being a lot of fun, not knowing that there would be difficult times ahead. Most important, the summer initiated the close and fun relationship I would always have with my oldest sister, Kathryn.

Most of the money I earned went toward the purchase of clothes and a watch with my name engraved on the backside of it. A jewelry store in Roswell had let me pay five dollars a week on it, and after each weekly payday at Safeway I went in to pay on the watch. By the time I was ready to leave Roswell I had become a proud owner of a Bulova watch. The watch was certainly a cut above the Waltham I had purchased in Baltimore, Maryland, during my high school trip to the East coast. This watch was my most expensive and treasured possession up to this point in my life.

I returned home at the end of the summer and spent about a week with my parents getting ready for my next new adventure, one which would require major changes to the types of social

Chapter 8 Summer, 1958 I

relationships I had been used to. With the exception of my Roswell experience, my entire life had been spent living and interacting mostly with fellow Indians. In spite of this, I was not anticipating any problems adjusting to a completely new environment.

My parents borrowed $200.00 for me. They also bought me a suit, and I either purchased a footlocker, or one of my siblings gave me theirs. I packed my linen and the few clothes I had purchased. At Ganado we changed one sheet per week by replacing the bottom sheet with the top one, which I planned to do at Emporia.

Kendall Hall, College of Emporia

Chapter 9
College Years Part I, 1958 – 1960

College of Emporia, Kansas

I imagine it was at Daniel's suggestion that I decided to go by train from Albuquerque to Emporia. I figured that if I left Albuquerque in late afternoon I would arrive at Emporia early the following morning. I wanted to arrive early in the day in order to have plenty of time to find my way around, to register, and most importantly, to get into the dormitory and have access to the dining hall.

In early September, 1958, I once again left my family to continue my journey, one that was going to be quite different, and one I would be traveling by myself. Up to this time I had entered new situations when I had my siblings with me or was in a setting that was predominantly Indian.

Emporia, Kansas was now going to be the farthest in distance I would be from home. For the first time I had to take into consideration my finances. I don't remember whether I worried about making it in college, or really what I thought about as I rode the train to Emporia. I'm sure I was apprehensive about what I would find after getting there, but I was anxious to get started. This was my first time traveling by train, and I really didn't get to see much as the sun set not too long after leaving Albuquerque. I was due to arrive in Emporia around five o'clock the following morning, and my plans were to remain at the train depot until the offices opened at the school.

I was able to sleep off and on during the night, and I did not wake up until after the train went past Emporia. The conductor said I could get off at the next stop, which was Topeka, about sixty miles away, and catch the first westbound train back to Emporia. I arrived

Right Place, Right Time

in Topeka as it was getting light. After arranging for my return trip, I had time before I would catch the next train back to Emporia.

Since I had not eaten since the previous day, I decided to find a place to eat breakfast. I went outside the depot and spotted a diner about a block away. I walked over there, went in, and found a place to sit at the counter. Even though the waiters were going back and forth in front of me waiting on the other people, none would wait on me. Finally, I asked one of them if they would wait on me. He said, "wait a minute", left and went back into the kitchen. He came back out and told me that they couldn't serve me or words to that effect. I got up and left. I walked back to the depot to wait for the train to take me back to Emporia.[20]

As I think back on that particular incident I've often wondered how I was able to proceed with my plans to go back to Emporia and enroll. I don't recall getting scared at what happened. I guess I was just too naïve to be scared. I don't recall anyone ever telling me that something like this could happen. It was probably best this way; otherwise it could have possibly affected my decision about going away to college.

I was glad to just get back on the train and to get out of Topeka, hoping that the college would be like Ganado since it was a Presbyterian-affiliated school. I must have taken a taxi from the train depot to the campus which was not that far away. I checked into the dorm and was assigned a second floor room located at one end of the two story men's dorm. I soon met another freshman who was from Pennsylvania, and he and I walked around exploring the campus that day. The day that began badly ended well, and my optimism returned as I began getting acquainted with other students and had a place to live. So began my life as a college student.

The College of Emporia, which closed in 1973, was a small liberal arts college with an enrollment of 300-350 students during my two years, which was not a whole lot bigger than Ganado's

Chapter 9 College Years, Part I

enrollment. The campus consisted of no more than seven buildings that housed three dormitories, two classroom buildings, a library, a dining room in the basement of the women's dorm, gymnasium, and an athletic field. It also had a grave yard where we "buried" teams we had defeated.[21]

The majority of the students were from Kansas and the neighboring states. There were a number of foreign students. The ones I remember were mostly from Iran and Cuba. In fact my roommate the first year was an Iranian, Ali.

Menaul School in Albuquerque had several of its graduates attending. One of its former students, an All-State New Mexico high school football player, was my dorm's barber who cut my hair for, I believe, $2.00 or $3.00. He and I once bet on a ping pong game, and I was able to win a free haircut from him, the first and only time we placed a bet involving a free haircut. I didn't blame him as I believe this was how he was supporting himself.

I remember very little about the first few weeks except for the freshmen initiation activities, such as having to wear a Beanie and being taken through the city park blindfolded, etc. I was shy and so unsure of myself that the initiation was embarrassing and very uncomfortable for me. I was relieved after it was over with. It's interesting that I don't recall anything about the initiation of the incoming freshmen when I returned for my sophomore year.

My first years' experience in college was probably similar in many ways to those of other freshmen. However I immediately felt a deep sense of isolation even though my dorm mates were friendly and we freshmen boys hung around together. The most obvious reason for my sense of isolation had to do with the fact that there were only two of us who were Native Americans. The other student was an Alaskan Native. She was a senior, and I was too timid to even try to strike up a conversation with her.

Right Place, Right Time

I had a real hard time relating to the other students other than my dorm mates. Even the basics of striking up conversations were really hard for me, which I had not previously experienced. I had always been quiet, but I had never experienced any difficulty entering into conversations. It became obvious to me fairly quickly that in order for me to fit in socially I'd have to take the initiative to converse with others. I couldn't. So my school life started off uncomfortably and pretty much stayed that way throughout the first year, improving somewhat the second year.

I felt real backward. While my dorm mates talked about getting dates and looking forward to various campus events, I seemed to spend my time thinking about what was I going to do, or finding other boys who might be in the same boat socially. Luckily I found a core of freshmen to hang out with.

This inability to converse, or lacking the confidence to try, affected my participation in class discussions. I rarely spoke up in class. I attended all my classes, and when my classes were dismissed, I either headed to my next class, or I returned to the dorm to study. While I did above average work in most of my classes, I failed miserably in my science and math classes. Here, these were the classes where I had been successful in high school. I'm sure the instructors would have helped me if I had asked. I could have also arranged for a tutor myself. I did neither. I don't remember whether it was because I didn't think of it, or I just didn't know any better.

There were several classes of which I have fun memories. As a part of a Biology class, the students were required to set up an aquarium and to bring it to class once a week to show how each of us were maintaining them. I couldn't keep my fish alive, and several times during that semester I had to catch a ride to the store where I had bought the fish to buy replacements to take to class. Other than that class, I was honest in carrying out my assignments. I could have

Chapter 9 College Years, Part I

had an excuse that I came from the desert part of the country and was unfamiliar with what was required in caring for fish.

Another class I remember was the Religion class. This class again seemed to be a progression of my religious training I had received at home and at Ganado. At least for this one class, I felt pretty comfortable in it. The professor had a unique system of grading papers. If a student, say, scored an 89 on a paper or an exam, she would write on the paper, "--- a B+, almost an A-", etc.

I took German as my foreign language course because my friend, Ted, was either taking the same class, or he had already taken it, so I saw him as a ready source of help. I should have taken Spanish instead, as it would have been more useful to me coming from New Mexico. I got a B out of the class. Close to the Christmas season we learned the words to *O Tannenbaum, O Christmas Tree*, and we tried hard to sing it in class. If my grade had been dependent on my singing, I would not have done well.

Another funny new experience I had was in my freshmen physical education class. We had a section on wrestling. The only kind of wrestling I was familiar with was the professional wrestling I had seen where the wrestlers went after each other immediately and threw around folding chairs, etc. I learned that in amateur wrestling, the match began with the two wrestlers on the floor side by side on their hands and knees. At least this was the way the instructor showed us how to wrestle. I thought what a strange way to wrestle. I also learned that the amateur wrestlers did not throw chairs or create mayhem off the mat.

My other major area of concentration throughout my four years in college was working to earn spending money. Practically every Saturday I worked at odd jobs in Emporia. One Friday night several of us had stayed up all night playing Pitch, a popular card game, quitting only in time to go to breakfast. I had planned to go to bed after breakfast. When I got back to the dorm, I learned I had a

Right Place, Right Time

job that morning. Since I couldn't afford not to take it, I went to work spending the day hauling dirt in a wheelbarrow.

There were other students who had to work. There was a Hispanic student from a small village in Northern New Mexico who worked really hard. He worked as a busboy in a local hotel restaurant. There were other students who worked in the kitchen and other places on campus. I always thought that the other guy from New Mexico and I were the most needy as I don't think either of us got much money from home.

Eventually I got a steady Saturday job working at a plant nursery owned by the spouse of a college employee. Each Saturday morning the owner picked me up and drove me out to his nursery which was located in rural Emporia. I helped him with his nursery chores, and one day we transplanted hundreds of strawberry plants. Then we had to pick the fruit after they ripened. This was the first time I had eaten strawberries, and I ate so many that I didn't crave them for many years.

The couple was really good to me. She worked half days on Saturdays, and when she got home at noon she always fixed us a good lunch of hamburger steak. During the time I was working for him, I had a chance to catch a ride home to New Mexico during spring break. When I told him, he was happy for me, and he even paid me for that one day I didn't work.

Up until this point in my life I had avoided the use of alcohol by staying away from people who used it. I imagine my mother's feelings against drinking had a lot to do with it, and I was never tempted. I had seen the effects of uncontrolled drinking on several members of my family, and that had some influence on me. This changed after I entered college, and I imagine it had to do with wanting to be accepted. There were a few "experienced" drinkers, but most of us seemed to be newcomers to this activity. This mainly took place on weekends at the popular student tavern. This was not

Chapter 9 College Years, Part I

a weekly activity; nor do I remember it as ever becoming problematic for any of us.

I was always careful about staying out of trouble. I once had to break away from a group I was with after leaving the tavern because of their boisterousness. I was afraid we would get picked up by the police. Occasionally we had a designated driver transport us back to the campus. Even in the late 1950's we already thought about getting designated drivers.

There were fun activities that I participated in, such as traveling to away athletic events with other students. Once a group of us drove to see a Kansas City Athletics baseball game. As we were waiting to cross a street in mid-town, we were evidently standing off the curb. A passing driver yelled at us, "You're in the city now, boys!" Another late night activity was eating at one of the favorite student eating places, Blaylock's Restaurant, when we were able to get one of the car owners to drive us.

During my first year a number of my former schoolmates were attending the government vocational school, Haskell Institute, in Lawrence, Kansas, which is near Emporia. I took a bus to Lawrence to visit a Ganado classmate, Bradley, over a weekend. My friend put a mattress on the floor in his room for me to sleep on. While there I also got to see several of my Paguate Day School classmates. Over the weekend Bradley and I attended the KU Relays, which at the time was one of the premier track meets in the country.

It was really nice to spend time with fellow Indians. Haskell reminded me of my Ganado Mission days, but the campus atmosphere was too much like what I remembered about the Albuquerque Indian School. The campus buildings were the typical government-built structures, and one of the men's dorms was located underneath the stands of their stadium. I enjoyed my weekend with my friends, yet I was glad to get back despite my own struggles about fitting in.

Right Place, Right Time

I attended church sporadically. There was not a church on campus, and a few of us would attend a Presbyterian church in town on occasion. After I got to Tulsa, I attended an Indian church once. The part the church had previously played in my life was now missing. I missed going to church as I always felt good when I did attend. I was too unsure of myself to attend church by myself.

I was always able to go home during school breaks, except for the first Thanksgiving break when my friend, Ted, invited me to go home with him. Ted was from Ponca City, Oklahoma. It was during this visit that he and I, along with his high school friends who were attending Oklahoma State, went to the Oklahoma Sooners and Oklahoma State  football game in Stillwater. This holiday visit also began my lifelong friendship with his wonderful family.

The second Thanksgiving a classmate from Bayfield, Colorado and I caught a ride with two other classmates, one of whom was from Tucumcari, NM. After getting to Tucumcari, we caught a bus to Albuquerque where I got off, and she continued on to Bayfield. We reversed our travel back to Tucumcari after spending no more than a day and a half with our families in order to get back to school on time.

Chapter 9 College Years, Part I

My first year was especially lonely at Emporia. The one way I dealt with this loneliness was to sleep in the afternoons. Since I didn't have any afternoon classes, I ate lunch and went back to my room and slept. Sleeping didn't help me much as I always felt worse after waking up. To this day, I rarely take a nap during the day, other than dozing off in a chair, because of this experience that occurred many years ago. As I think about my first year at Emporia, it is that terrible feeling of loneliness that I recall most vividly. Fortunately it eased somewhat as the year went by.

I've wondered how I was able to "hang in there" and continue in school when things were not going well for me. I received poor grades in my area of interest, compounded by problems of adjustment. To top off all these problems, I just barely had enough money to make ends meet. Fortunately, the one thought that evidently never entered my mind was quitting school. Not quitting was one of the characteristics of the Carr children, a valuable lesson we evidently learned from our parents.

Evelyn talked about her difficulties in college, and quitting never entered her mind either. Daniel even dropped out of school after his first year at Emporia and joined the Navy. After his discharge he returned to the University of New Mexico and graduated. Maybe the thought of herding sheep was enough to keep me in school. After I completed my first year, as difficult as it had been, I knew I was going to return for my sophomore year.

I took the bus home at the end of my first year. On the bus ride home I happened to sit next to a man who had a road map, and every so often he would take it out and study it. I finally asked him if I could look at it. His response, "No, you might tear it!" On that note, my first year of college came to a close.

Right Place, Right Time

Summer at Home, 1959

After completing each of my two years at Emporia I returned home for the summer. When I returned home after my freshman year, I was really quite proud of myself for making it through my first year in view of my problems of adjusting to college life. In fact I felt pretty special as I was one of only a handful of local young people who had returned home for the summer from other schools of higher learning.

Most of my brothers and sisters happened to be away this summer. Evelyn had already completed her first full year of teaching at the government day school at McCartys on the Pueblo of Acoma Reservation. This summer she was attending summer school at Colorado State College in Greeley, working on her Master's Degree in Elementary Education. Daniel was in the Navy. Kathryn was away at some military base with her family. Alice and her family lived in Kingman, Arizona where her husband taught school and she worked as a nurse. Edna and her husband were living in Guishsche, and Elgin lived in Albuquerque with his family. I just don't remember Walter being at home that summer. He was going be a senior in high school that fall.

One evening I was walking through the village when I ran into several of my former schoolmates from the day school, sitting outside the store which had closed for the day. One of them was my best day school friend. He and I were the ones who took our classmates on the end-of-school-picnic in our grandfathers' horse-pulled wagons. I spoke to them, and he asked me where I had been as he had not seen me in some time. When I told him I had just returned from college, he responded, Gaamu, tuuna trusumashta. Gaamu is an expression of envy that I was still going to school. My friend made a career serving in the U. S. Navy, from which he eventually retired.

Chapter 9 College Years, Part I

Going to different boarding schools and our lives taking different directions, did not help in reestablishing the day school friendships. I had also started on my summer job with the Anaconda Mining Company, the operator of the Jackpile uranium mine on the outskirts of the village. The tribe had arranged with the company to provide summer employment for those students who were attending college.

There were about seven of us students who were hired, three of us from Guishsche. We spent the summer painting the interior of the homes in the housing compound for employees of the Anaconda Company. Our boss was a local school employee who was off for the summer. We were organized, and we did become good painters. I don't recall any of us missing work. Only one time did several of us barely make it to work on time. We had to drive directly to work after returning from the annual 4th of July weekend Indian Pow-Wow in Flagstaff, Arizona.

Working at the mine helped me establish new friendships, and the fact that we were all in college made a difference. This summer job gave me an opportunity to meet and work with several of the guys who were from the other villages. In fact I did not know any of them, even though two of them were from my village. They had lived elsewhere throughout the time I was still living at home.

While all the Laguna villages are located within about a twelve mile radius of each other, the fact that we did not have transportation minimized inter-village associations. About the only tribal events I remember attending away from my village were the Laguna feast on September 19th and one or two ceremonial events, also at Laguna.

Spending summers at the sheep camp also limited the opportunities for meeting young people from the other villages. Boarding school and my employment at the mine were the first opportunities I had for meeting other young people.

Right Place, Right Time

I enjoyed my summer as I formed new friendships within my tribe. I was happy to be home and to have a chance to "recover" from the difficulties at college. I was able to see that I was maturing and was developing into a pretty responsible individual. At least I thought I was, particularly with my employment. I was also proud of the fact that I was now earning my own money and saving it for my clothes and school expenses

Guishsche Undergoing Major Changes

The summer of 1959 was the first time I had spent an entire summer at home since leaving for boarding school in 1952. When I had returned home after my first year at Ganado, I could see that some changes were beginning to take place in the lives of the villagers. When I returned home after my first year in college, I noticed that some major changes had taken place involving our traditional way of life.

Since these were the days before the initiation of the federal government's Housing and Urban Development built homes, the mud plastered homes still looked the same. The village "streets" were still unpaved, but what was inside most of the houses, including my parents', had changed: TV sets, refrigerators, and new furniture. Vehicles were now parked in front of many of the homes. TV antennas were sprouting from practically every roof top. This was long before cable television, so the programs we watched were limited to what was produced by the three networks.

Even though I had spent parts of the summers at home between 1952 and 1958, I was too young to observe the changes that were beginning to take place. The discovery and the mining of uranium had brought to a close in a most significant way many of our traditional ways of life.

For the first time most of the people had income. They were now able to purchase automobiles and were able to travel wherever

Chapter 9 College Years, Part I

and whenever they wanted to go. Transportation opened up a whole new spectrum of recreational choices which didn't exist during my pre-boarding school days. Electricity brought about television and replaced battery operated radios. Life became more sedentary. Farming and sheep herding became secondary. In fact, this may have been the time sheep owners began switching to cattle, as cattle work was not as labor-intensive as raising sheep.

I believe the ownership of vehicles, in particular, made a major difference in our lifestyle. People were now in a hurry to get to places, and this reduced the interactions that had been possible when people were still walking. The time that used to be taken to exchange greetings had basically stopped. It became too inconvenient to stop the vehicle to greet people who were walking or riding in other vehicles. As a result a lot of the interpersonal communication was reduced to a wave of the hand.

I can't say that old ways of interacting with each other had completely gone by the wayside, but it did appear that it was no longer a common practice. However, today driving on the State road between K'awaika and Guishsche, I still see drivers waving even if they don't know who they are waving to. I think this is quite unique in our fast-paced world. I still wave when I am driving on this road, a habit I'm glad I haven't lost.

The interdependence of the people suffered. It felt like everyone was now on their own. Before, there was always the feeling that we looked after one another, which served as a valuable safety net for us. During the time I was growing up people volunteered to help without expecting anything in return. Now it appeared this had changed, or the former practices were not so obvious anymore. If one needed transportation, one now was expected to pay for it.

Even my family was undergoing changes. Dad had gone to work as a laborer with a company involved with the uranium mining

Right Place, Right Time

activity. Even though his work site was a few miles from the house, Evelyn said he just walked to work even though he had a vehicle by then. One of my sisters thought that he had been encouraged by one of our sisters to obtain the job in order to be eligible for Social Security benefits in his later years.

He still had his flock of sheep, but now he had someone caring for them. He still spent all his spare time overseeing their care. During the summer months when the days are longer, he would go to his sheep camp to check on his herder and flock. He returned to his original livelihood after he retired from his employment.

There were now a few organized activities for the young people, such as dances and baseball teams on the reservation. The teams competed against each other and were made up of mostly young adults. One of the summers at home, I played on the team from my village. This activity again provided me with additional opportunity to get to know more people from the reservation.

There were some really good athletes who, with proper training and instruction, might have been able to excel even more. Two local boys later became outstanding football players for their schools, one in an Albuquerque public school and the other one at the local high school. Both were recognized for their talents. There was a local Catholic priest, Father Kenneth, I believe was his name, who was quite a baseball player and played for one of the teams.

Even the type of food we ate had changed. This was especially noticeable from the lunches my mother prepared for me to take to work. Before, a bologna sandwich made with store-bought bread and mayonnaise was a special treat. Now it was practically an everyday lunch staple. Soft drinks were now an everyday beverage and no longer limited to special occasions. Our meals at home remained basically the same, although store-

Chapter 9 College Years, Part I

purchased foods were now becoming a part of our everyday diet, and we had more access to store bought snacks.

English was beginning to replace some of our everyday native language in the home. We still spoke primarily in Laguna. However, the use of English was now a part of the everyday language, particularly among my age group. The change from the use of Laguna to English I feel severely impacted our cultural practices. It especially affected the interpersonal communications and relationships that had perpetuated the common values and traditions of the tribe.

The most obvious change to me was this whole area of acknowledging people's presence as a way of showing respect, particularly those involving the elders. Much later, my sister told me of a man lamenting about how the young people today no longer practiced this manner of addressing elders. She quoted him saying, "All they know how to say is "Hi." By 1959 the traditional ways of dealing with relationships were changing.

Changes were also taking place in my relationship with my parents. I was now nineteen years of age and had already been living away from home for close to seven years, and I had become pretty independent. My folks respected my independence, yet I felt I was still accountable to them. I didn't contribute financially, but I made a special effort to help them in other ways, especially by trying to stay out of trouble.

What had not changed was the usual reminder when I left the house to go out with my friends. Tramee weh knaknetra dya sru, telling me to behave myself.

Sophomore Year, 1959 - 1960

As much as I had enjoyed my summer at home, I was ready to return to Emporia in September. I also looked forward to returning as my good friend, Ted, and I were going to be roommates.

Right Place, Right Time

I didn't get lonesome the second year. I still was not able to participate in class, or for that matter, to interact with others in group settings. However this did not get me down as much. Overall, I got to feeling better, and I did not feel quite as isolated as I did the year before.

I did have to begin thinking about what to major in. I felt it was no longer realistic about becoming an engineer due to my poor grades in math and the sciences. The most important goal for me, however, was just to get a degree. I had not given much thought to what else I wanted to major in, yet I had to find an area in which to concentrate. For lack of any other ideas, I thought about Education as being a possibility. Anyway, I still had to concentrate on my basic course requirements, so I was able to put off this decision for the time being.

I continued to work on weekends. My life was still limited to studying, going to classes, and hanging out mostly with the guys. I was always on the lookout for part-time work. In spite of these limitations I enjoyed my second year. I found various ways to get home during school breaks. My visits home always gave me renewed strength to continue my efforts as everyone was always happy to see me, and I felt they were proud of me

I don't think I ever told my family about the difficulties I was experiencing at school. I felt that I could handle these problems without bothering them about it. Not worrying them was always in the back of my mind. Attending boarding school contributed greatly to my early independence, yet I am convinced that this was not the best way to grow up. However, these early experiences of being on my own helped me get through the difficult periods as I knew I had to succeed.

My family continued to provide me with the support I needed. I received occasional letters from them, always with encouraging words and their expression of love for me. I enjoyed

Chapter 9 College Years, Part I

writing letters with detailed descriptions of my activities. I remember how proud I was buying a box of stationary that had my school's "Fighting Presbies" logo on the letterhead which I used for my letters home. At the time letters were my only contacts with my family.

Daniel, who was now in the Navy, surprised me early one morning with his visit. He was en route to his new assignment in California after completing his specialized training in Virginia Beach, Virginia. He and a friend were driving cross country, stopping to see me early one morning. He stopped for only a few minutes, and he left me twenty dollars. I'll never forget how much this short stop meant to me. It was winter time when they came through, and he told me later that the car heater was not working. Driving cross-country through the Midwest in mid-winter without a working heater had to be pretty brutal.

Having a close friend like Ted helped me. Ted had led me to believe that he knew how to fix grilled cheese sandwiches and that we would be eating a lot of them in the course of the year. He came back with a hot plate from home that his dad had gotten him, along with a metal plate on which to fix the sandwiches. I don't know if Ted forgot how to fix the sandwiches. Unless my memory has failed me completely, I don't recall eating many grilled cheese sandwiches, if any. Anyway, Ted had fallen in love that year, and he didn't have the time to be fixing grilled cheese sandwiches.

Decision to Transfer

In the spring of my sophomore year in 1960 a group of us were out on a Friday night drinking beer when the conversation turned to possibly transferring to other schools. During the discussion one guy and I decided to drive to Tulsa, Oklahoma, close to two hundred miles away, to enroll at the University of Tulsa. Just like that.

Right Place, Right Time

I don't even remember why we chose Tulsa. I had only been to Tulsa and the University campus once before in 1956 when I took the cross-country trip. We had stopped there to visit a former school mate of ours. Other than that visit, all I knew about the school was that it was a Presbyterian-related university and that it had a pretty campus.

Anyway we left for Tulsa in the middle of that same night, arriving in town early Saturday morning. The school's business office must have been open on Saturday mornings as we picked up the application forms for enrollment. We spent the night in the local YMCA and returned to Emporia the following day.

Ted and Me Today

With that spur-of-the-moment decision, I must have felt that I was ready to move on. I applied to Tulsa for admission and was accepted. I may have been prompted to transfer as my friend Ted was going to marry that summer and he and his future wife, Mary, a school mate, were going to transfer to Morningside College in Sioux City, Iowa.

Chapter 9 College Years, Part I

It is doubtful that I consulted my parents about these plans to transfer. I was pretty much on my own already, and I had basically assumed all the financial responsibilities for my schooling. As I think about this independence and making major decisions on my own, I've often wondered how my parents felt. Did they feel left out, or were they glad that I was able to make it on my own. We never discussed things of this nature. However, I always sensed that they were pretty proud of all their children who all seemed capable of making rational decisions about their lives. I may have been the exception, in view of how I made my decision to transfer to the University of Tulsa.

A classmate offered me a ride home when my second school year ended. He was from Tucson, Arizona. We must have left Emporia late afternoon, and we drove all night, or Bill did, as he did all the driving. Someplace in the northwest Texas Panhandle, he dozed off. The car left the highway, and we woke up as the car was heading up a shallow incline. Other than this incident, we made it safely the rest of the way. Bill was kind enough to go eight miles out of his way to deliver me to my front door.

Last Summer Living at Home, 1960

By the second summer I had become even more independent. I was also more aware of how hard my parents worked, and my respect for my parents continued to grow. I thought the least I could do was to stay out of trouble and try to meet their expectations. I continued to try to be as helpful as I could be to them. Like the previous summer, I didn't contribute financially so I saved most of my earnings for clothes and for my spending money at school.

There were times I didn't get home until way late at night on weekends, but I still got up when my folks did. Nobody ever slept late in our household, or dared to. My early rising, generally before

Right Place, Right Time

sunrise, has stayed with me to this day. I've placed all the blame for my inability to sleep late on my sheepherding days, my boarding school days, and my parents.

I ran around a great deal more with some of the guys I worked with at the mine and with their friends. One of the guys owned a car, a convertible, which took us many places that summer, mostly into Albuquerque or to the other villages on weekends. My dad would have let me use his truck too, but my friends would not have wanted to sit in the back of the truck.

The guys I worked with at the mine were a mix in terms of their participation in the cultural practices. I happened to be one who had never participated in the tribe's religious ceremonial activities and knew next to nothing about them. There were one or two who were more deeply involved in them and another one who was pretty active in the Pow-Wows.

The guy who owned the convertible always had a drum in his car, and when my friends got the urge to sing, they would get the drum out and break out with Indian songs. When we were returning from Flagstaff late that one night, it was their drumming and singing that kept us awake. I never joined them in the singing as I didn't know any of the songs, much less know how to sing. This never bothered them.

This particular summer I went to visit my former classmates from Ganado out on the Hopi Reservation in Arizona. I took a Greyhound bus from Laguna to Gallup, New Mexico, about ninety miles away. From there I hitchhiked and caught two rides to Ganado, which is fifty three miles from Gallup. One of my former classmates was working there for the summer, and I talked him into accompanying me to Hopi Land the next day in his car.

I asked the housemother if I could spend the night in the dorm. I did have to go to bed when it was time for the students to go to bed as the lights would be going out. After we all got into bed,

Chapter 9 College Years, Part I

the housemother came in and began reading them their bed time story! I lay in bed quietly laughing at myself thinking, a college sophomore still being read a bedtime story.

It was worth it as I had a bed to sleep in that night, and I was able to eat in the dining hall. The Mission personnel remained as welcoming as they were when I first arrived there as a seventh grader.

After visiting friends at Hopi, my friend drove me back to Gallup to catch a bus back to Laguna. On the bus ride home I ran into another former schoolmate, which made this a fun weekend. By the time I got off the bus at Laguna it was already night time. Since there was little or no traffic that late at night, I had to walk all eight miles back home. Back then it was relatively safe to hitchhike, and we were able to get around without our own means of transportation. My weekend trip to Arizona is a good example.

We ended our summer employment with a party in the canyon west of Guishsche. We had had a busy summer, working and going out, often times together on weekends. These two summers had been good for me as I got to know people from the other villages as well as the guys I worked with. Not all of us returned to college; nor did all of us graduate. However, all of us found ways to "give back" for the opportunity the tribe gave us by working out this arrangement with Anaconda.

Several of the guys became quite active in tribal government. One eventually served in several elected positions, including multiple terms as tribal Governor. This particular individual is a good example of how it is possible to live a traditional way of life, yet be able to move comfortably between our two worlds very successfully. I'm afraid there are too many people who still believe it has to be one or the other.

Rather than returning to Emporia in September, I headed for the University of Tulsa. This second summer at home in 1960 was

Right Place, Right Time

really the last time I lived with my parents. I was planning to return the following summer because of the job at the mine. However, by the time summer arrived, I had to remain in Tulsa to attend summer school. By then I was also working part time regularly.

However, Guishsche has always remained my home. When I'm asked today where I'm from, I always say I'm from the Pueblo of Laguna and from the village of Guishsche. It was my family and the local people who gave me the tools to venture out into the world with confidence. As I got ready to leave again, I looked forward to another set of experiences in a different school and city. I was now quite confident that I would succeed even though my familiarity with Tulsa consisted of only two prior visits.

All my tuition and fees for my third year were covered by scholarships. As a result, I had put my summer earnings toward clothes and my school expenses. I knew I wanted to complete college, so I was ready for another school year.

Tulsa YMCA

Where I Intended to Stay Temporarily

Chapter 10
College Years Part II
1960 - 1962

New City and School

When I had applied for admission to the university the previous spring I evidently did not indicate that I wanted to live in the dorm. It may have been an oversight, or else I had decided not to live in a dorm, I don't remember. Anyway, I left for Tulsa, Oklahoma by bus, not having a prearranged place to live. My plans were to stay at the YMCA until I found a place. As with my planned early arrival in Emporia two years earlier, I made sure I arrived in Tulsa early in the day to give me time to find my way around and hopefully find a place to live.

I found my way from the bus depot to the YMCA in downtown Tulsa. I guess I never thought about what if the YMCA did not have a room available. Luckily, it did. I paid for one or two weeks in advance, not knowing how long it would take me to find a permanent place to live. I checked into my room, a small dimly-lit room with a single bed, a bedside stand, and a chest of drawers. I immediately knew I didn't want to stay here very long. The room was too depressing. I deposited my footlocker in the room, got directions to the university campus and caught a city bus to my new school.

As I walked through the administration building I just happened to notice a bulletin board that had ads for off-campus housing. I spotted an ad for a boarding house which I thought would be within walking distance of the campus. I recognized the street name, Sixth Street, as the one I had just come on my way to the campus. I hurriedly walked to the boarding house, a two-story, well-maintained residence. A bed was available for $75.00 per month that included breakfast and dinner.

Right Place, Right Time

As soon as I paid a month's rent, I rushed back by bus to the YMCA to check back out, and I was able to get a full refund. I was settled in the boarding house by dinner time of my first day in Tulsa, Oklahoma. From that first evening meal on, I watched "Highway Patrol" on a small black and white TV as I and the other boarders ate dinner.

There were about seven boarders, all of whom were older than me. One was permanently employed and had been a long-time resident. There was one other university student who came to live there, a Canadian. The others were all attending a local school of aviation for advanced pilot training. One of them owned a plane.

I felt real comfortable with them right away. Other than the employed resident, we spent most weekday evenings studying. Later on, when we finished studying or when we got tired of studying, we would occasionally walk down to the corner tavern and have a beer before heading back to bed. On the weekends everybody went about their business. On occasion I went out with some of them. Since they usually went to night clubs, I passed on these outings since I didn't dance.

The University of Tulsa Experience

I walked about five or six blocks to school daily, and sometimes I did some of my studying at the university library. Since all the boarders were gone during the day time, the boarding house was a good place to study as it was quiet. I had gotten a scholarship from my tribe for either my first or second year at Tulsa as they now had a scholarship

University of Tulsa

Chapter 10 College Years, Part II

program using the proceeds from the uranium mine. I've always thought that I got a favorable response to my scholarship application as one of the students I worked with at the mine was now a tribal official. This scholarship was in addition to my Board of National Missions scholarship so I was not in dire straits financially anymore.

I looked around on campus hoping to spot other Indian students without much success. Long after I graduated I met a guy, a Pawnee, who happened to have been a student there at the same time. He had lived in the dorm and was an engineering student. There was another Indian student who played quarterback for the football team. He was an Osage. I never got to meet him, but I kind of used him as a role model. I thought if he could succeed in the classroom as well as an athlete at the college level, I could too, at least in the classroom.

I went to all of our home games. One of them was against the New Mexico State Aggies. This was in 1960 when the Aggies were undefeated. That was also the year they had the three stars, Pervis Atkins, Bob Gaithers, and Charley Johnson. Their winning streak was still intact after we played them.

At that time football at Tulsa had not become a big time sport as it is today. They played their games in Skelly Stadium, a Tulsa public school stadium. There would usually be only a small cluster of fans at the games. Since that time in 1960, that stadium has been transformed into a beautiful multimillion dollar stadium, and Tulsa now plays power house teams like the University of Oklahoma and other major universities.

By the time I arrived in Tulsa, I had become close friends with my friend Ted's family, Mr. and Mrs. Roy Garten, Junior, and his sister, Nancy. Beginning with that first visit in their home in Ponca City during the Thanksgiving break in 1958, Ted's family made me feel as if I had known them forever. So it was through my friendship with the Garten family that I learned about the field of social work as

Right Place, Right Time

Mrs. Garten was a former child welfare worker for the State of Oklahoma. My interest in social work grew the more I learned about it.

As a result of this new found interest, I declared Sociology as my major and Psychology as my minor. My grades became A's and B's. The hardest course I took was Economics because I had difficulty understanding the subject. The professor also used what he described as the Socratic method of teaching. Each student was required to ask a question during class for purposes of discussion. Since turns came according to alphabetical order, I skipped class on the days I knew my name would be coming up. Since it was a large class, I was able to stay within the allowed limit for "cutting" class.

I was still plagued about not being able to speak up in class so I always enrolled in large classes where there was the least likelihood of being called upon by the professor. I knew those days would soon be coming to an end as the social work-related classes were very small and I would need to begin taking part in class. While I never became a very active participant in class discussions, at least I began to speak up. The small class size helped me immensely, and the professor was very supportive. The fact that my classmates were all focusing on a similar field made a difference for me in trying to take part in conversations and discussions.

It was in one of these social work classes in my second year that I first met my future wife, Patricia Merriman, a local non-Indian student. She had transferred to Tulsa that year from the Oklahoma Baptist University where she had attended her freshmen year. I was a senior at that time. I eventually gained up enough courage to ask her for a date. It may have been after she had stopped to offer me a ride as I was walking back to the boarding house from the campus. Dating Pat contributed mightily to the successful conclusion to my college career, and my eventual marriage to her continued that boundless love and support from her.

Chapter 10 College Years, Part II

Living and Working in Tulsa

I did have to continue working to supplement my scholarships. As soon as I got settled the first year, I began looking for part time work. Since the City of Tulsa was much bigger than Emporia, I was able to find employment fairly quickly.

The first temporary job I got was working as a driver for a business man who was blind. No, I did not wear a uniform, or a chauffeur's cap. I did drive him around in his Cadillac. He was in the grain market business. One time I drove him to a town just inside the Kansas border. On one stretch of road, he told me to lower the car window and to listen for a singing sound. I didn't hear anything that sounded like music. He said this stretch of road was called the "singing highway" or words to that effect.

Working for this business man was the first and last time I was privileged to drive a Cadillac. This job also gave me an opportunity to work with an individual who possessed a highly developed sense of where he was at the moment. He surprised me so many times with his directions, and what I should be alert to at a particular time and place. I left this job as it did not provide me with enough hours and earnings to supplement my scholarships. I was glad to have had this experience working for him.

I eventually got a job which was almost full time, going to work at three in the afternoon and getting off about nine at night. I worked at this job while taking a full load of courses. This was a dairy company that sold milk and ice cream from refrigerated trucks at a number of locations throughout the city. The customers drove up, and I took the product from the truck to their vehicles.

While working for this company it held a contest to see which location would show the greatest percentage sales increase during the designated contest period. I happened to have been assigned to one of the lower income neighborhood sites. Guess who won the contest? Yours truly won! It was a money prize which came

Right Place, Right Time

in handy. I worked at two different locations and Pat's family happened to purchase their milk from one of the locations that was close to their home. Pat would come by and purchase milk from me. I am sure I impressed her with my salesmanship, although she's never admitted it.

Since I needed this job, I remained in Tulsa during one of the Christmas breaks. All the residents at the boarding house, except me and another boarder, planned to return to their respective homes for the holidays, and the owners of the boarding house had also planned to be away. I was relieved that someone else would be there during Christmas. I got back to the boarding house after work on Christmas Eve, and the house was completely dark. Everybody had left town. This was the loneliest Christmas I've ever experienced.

There were also happy occasions. Just as he had appeared at Ganado when I needed a boost, The Reverend Roe B. Lewis made his second appearance while I was at Tulsa. He was working for the Board of National Indian Missions of the United Presbyterian Church as an educational counselor.[22] He came to visit me as I was one of his program's scholarship recipients, and he had come to offer his support as well as to monitor my progress. I really enjoyed his visit since I already knew him, and I had also been friends with one of his sons through my Westminster Fellowship activities.

In fact, during summer school I happened to be walking across the campus when I noticed an Indian guy walking toward me. As we met we looked at each other, and here it was one of Reverend Lewis' other sons. A real shocker, as I did not know he was attending summer school at Tulsa. I've thought of Reverend Lewis' visit many times and saw it as confirmation of the church's commitment to me and how it continued to offer its guidance and support even after leaving Ganado.

Chapter 10 College Years, Part II

My overall experience at the University and living in Tulsa was a lot better and much happier than my initial two years at Emporia. I began making friends, and my financial situation improved as a result of my scholarships and my jobs. There were periods between jobs when my finances suffered. But overall I was able to meet my living expenses. It was tough my final summer when I was trying to complete my coursework.

I even had enough money to buy two used cars. No, not at the same time. Soon after I bought the first one, it began blowing smoke out the exhaust pipe when the accelerator was pressed. The second one developed a gear problem so that I couldn't put it in reverse, much to the embarrassment of my girlfriend, now my wife, Pat. If I had to back up, I had to make sure that the car could roll backwards. A lot of my hard earned money went into purchasing an oil additive that was touted to stop the car from using oil between changes. My car must have been in pretty bad shape as the additive didn't make any difference in the amount of oil it used.

You may wonder how I could afford to buy gas with my limited resources. At the time, at least during the two years I spent in Tulsa, Regular gasoline sold on the average of twenty five cents a gallon. Many times there were "gas wars" that lowered the cost to about eighteen cents a gallon.

During my two years I was able to go home, catching rides with two of my fellow boarders and some friends. One Thanksgiving the guy who owned his own plane flew me to Albuquerque on his way home to Phoenix. This was the first time I had ever flown in a plane. He dropped me off in Albuquerque and picked me back up on his return on Sunday. This plane ride may have led me to eventually take flying lessons and earn a private pilot license.

Right Place, Right Time

Another time one of the other boarders, who was from the Amarillo, Texas, area, drove me as far as Amarillo where I caught a bus to Albuquerque. I met him back in Amarillo for the return to Tulsa. During one of the summers I spent in Tulsa, a friend and several of her friends were travelling to California, and I caught a ride with them to Laguna, returning to Tulsa on my own after a few days visiting my family.

My family was always glad to see me. They were impressed about how I got around, like catching rides home. Their reaction was always the word for being thankful, Dahwaeh, that someone was kind enough to give me a ride home. Catching rides was a whole new experience for my family and for me too. I'm certain they were proud of me. I was now able to make my way in a different kind of world than the one they were familiar with. I knew I was going to make it on my own. They had no need to worry about me as my self-confidence continued to grow.

Home Away from Home

In between visits home, I retreated to the Garten home in Ponca City when I got homesick, felt discouraged, or needed a boost. I've thought so many times about how fortunate I was having this relationship with the Gartens who lived only about 100 miles from Tulsa. Today I am embarrassed about my lack of sensitivity as I think

Chapter 10 College Years, Part II

back about how I often just showed up at their home without asking the family if it was all right to come visit. The family always welcomed me and was always happy to see me, just like my own family. Not one time did they make me feel that I was intruding.

Ted's father was Chief Engineer, Exploration-Geophysics, for Continental Oil Company whose headquarters were in Ponca City. As I mentioned earlier, Ted's mother had worked as a child welfare worker for the state's Child Welfare Division. Ted's younger sister, Nancy, was still in high school at the time. She then attended and graduated from Tulsa. She got her Masters in Social Work from the University of Oklahoma, and became a social worker like her mother. Ted and Mary were at Morningside College the two years I was at Tulsa, and I didn't get to see much of them.

Mr. and Mrs. Garten were very easy-going people, particularly Mr. Garten, and I felt very comfortable and relaxed around them. He was quiet and soft spoken, usually sitting back and letting Mrs. Garten do the talking. Mrs. Garten always wanted to know what was going on in my life. Was I going to church? How was school going? My work, etc. This made it extremely easy for me to talk, really to both of them.

Mrs. Garten often spoke of a tribe that lived near Ponca City, especially about how they were treated by the people in the community. It was never in a condescending way; rather as one who was sincere in trying to define what role she could play in the community's relationship with that particular tribe.

Both of them were very proud of being Oklahomans. She grew up in Guthrie, and Mr. Garten's family was from Piedmont, near Oklahoma City. During some of my visits they would take me on drives to show me some of the historic sites in and around Ponca City.

The Gartens had tremendous influence on me because of their kindness and how they made me feel about myself. Their faith

Right Place, Right Time

in God reminded me so much of my mother's faith. When I think about people of faith, I think of my mother and the Gartens.

Like my family, a portion of Sunday mornings with the Gartens was spent at their Presbyterian church. Both of them played various leadership roles, using their professional backgrounds in giving back to their church and to their community. Mr. Garten played a major role in the planning and construction of a beautiful assisted care facility in which both of them were able to reside later.

The longer I knew the Gartens, the more social work appealed to me. Mrs. Garten always spoke in such a caring and loving way about children and their families and how much she enjoyed her work. Since I was unfamiliar with the field of social work before meeting the Gartens, I've often wondered if I would have chosen this line of work if I had not met them. I always returned to Tulsa from my weekend visits feeling confident, happy, and I must say, well fed, and ready to continue my journey. I don't know what I would have done without the Gartens at the time.

I've given a lot of thought about why I became so "attached" to them. A great deal probably relates to my early departure from home and growing up in a boarding school. Before I matured enough to talk out issues with my parents, I was off to boarding school. So the kinds of relationships and communications that develop in families that remain intact, I never really developed. In fact boarding schools, even those as good as Ganado, do not provide the kind of environment that enhances the development of close relationships even though the staff made a tremendous effort to become good surrogate parents.

By the time I became acquainted with the Garten family, I had very little experience in sharing thoughts, ideas, or just conversing about events. Even getting immediate personal feedback was something I was not used to.

Chapter 10 College Years, Part II

It was these new experiences, plus the fact that feelings could be expressed verbally, that enhanced my feelings of closeness to the Gartens. Living far from my family made it difficult to maintain close contact with them as our primary means of communication was by mail. The Gartens, therefore, became my substitute parents, and I could have found no better substitutes than my dear friends.

Even after I left the state of Oklahoma, I stayed in touch with them. About every time I returned to the state, I took time to go visit them, as it was in their home that I always recharged myself. The Gartens made me feel so comfortable with them that I always hated to leave their home; just the same way I felt when I left my own home. In addition to their wonderful gift of friendship, my first credit card came from Mr. Garten. Yes, it was a Conoco card issued by his company. Among my most cherished gifts are the letters from Mrs. Garten, which remind me of the goodness of my dear friends, and which I still occasionally pull out today to reread.

Graduation in Sight – Spring, 1962

By the spring of my senior year I realized that I was going to lack the required number of credits to graduate in June and that I would have to attend summer school again. I would still lack three credits by the end of the summer session because some of my grades from Emporia didn't transfer.

I finally went to my counselor for advice as I could not afford to go another semester. She was very understanding about my predicament. I took the maximum hours allowable during summer school, and she arranged with another professor to allow me to do a small research project and write a paper for credit to make it possible for me to graduate at the end of summer school. To accomplish it, I had to give up my job with the milk company as I needed all the time to complete my studies and my paper.

Right Place, Right Time

It was worth it. I practically starved the last couple months of school as all I had left now was a small amount from my scholarships. Luckily Pat began inviting me to dinner with her family on Saturdays. Those meals were one of the few good weekly meals I ate during that last summer at Tulsa. I told Pat about this after we married. She said if she had known this she would have invited me more often. She was embarrassed that her family had beans for their meals a lot of the times I ate with them. Right next to my mother's, they were the best tasting beans.

When I first met her family, her father was working at two janitorial jobs, one during the day and one at night even though his health was not robust. Earlier on he had suffered from tuberculosis and had to be hospitalized, during which time the family was on public assistance. After his discharge from the hospital, he attended barber school, only able to remain in that line of work for a short period of time due to his diminished health.

So like my own family, the children began working early in their lives. My parents' resources were limited, yet I never felt we were poor. Pat says she knew they were poor, and judging from the stories she's shared with me, her family's resources were much more limited than ours.

Thankfully, the summer went by quickly. After four years of struggling financially, trying to fit in, and getting some failing grades, I reached my goal of actually getting a college degree. I was the second one, after Evelyn, to graduate. Daniel and Elgin got their degrees later. Alice was already a Registered Nurse by then, and Kathryn was already a Practical Nurse. In August, 1962, I graduated from the University of Tulsa with a Bachelor of Arts degree in Sociology, with a minor in Psychology.

I did not participate in TU's graduation ceremonies, nor did I feel that I was missing anything. I don't know if I got any congratulatory messages from home. I was really proud of myself

Chapter 10 College Years, Part II

for making it through college, although it had been difficult financially and socially. I had been so focused on surviving economically and getting a degree that all I must have thought about was that it was finally over, and I could now get a full time job.

The thought that kept me going throughout the four years was that if I could just get a degree, I would be able to get me a good job, which I did. I never gave much thought as to how far this education and my experiences would get me.

I know I missed out on many college experiences. I have to admit that I have always taken pride in the fact that I never had to be a financial burden to my parents after I got into college. I also take a great deal of pride in graduating from the University of Tulsa, a private school with an excellent reputation.

It is still difficult for me to fathom how my decision to transfer to Tulsa while I was out partying on a Friday night in Emporia, Kansas, translated into so many good things for me. Such as my friendship with the Garten family, meeting my future wife, professors who helped me graduate on time, and getting into the field of social work. To top it off, my first job was with a state agency that encouraged my graduate school education and paid for half of it. All this resulted from that one Friday night decision.

I've met a lot of wonderful people who were so good to me. Today, whenever I read in the newspaper about the numbers of people who respond to reports of tragedy with their generosity, I tell myself that I knew people like them.

Right Place, Right Time

Downtown Tulsa in the 1960s

postcards.bidstart.com
11/18/13

Chapter 11
Summer of Transition
College to First Job, 1962

Although my dear friend, Mrs. Garten never admitted it, I believe she had a hand in my getting my first job as a case-worker with the Child Welfare Division of the Oklahoma Department of Public Welfare. She had previously worked there and still had friends in that Department.

After completing my summer school classes, graduating, and getting the position with the Oklahoma Department of Public Welfare, I rushed home mainly to see if I could borrow my sister Evelyn's car temporarily as my smoke-blowing car wasn't fit for all the driving that was going to be required in my new job. I was completely broke by then, making it impossible to buy a better car.

Evelyn was in Greeley, Colorado that summer, finishing up her work on her Master's degree. When I got home my sister, Edna and her husband, Francis, drove me to Greeley to talk with my sister about borrowing her car temporarily. Like so many times before she came to my rescue and loaned me her car to take back to Oklahoma.

I returned to Oklahoma City for my two week orientation in the State's Public Welfare Department offices. I then moved to Enid, Oklahoma where I had been assigned to a district office that served several western Oklahoma counties. Before leaving for Enid, the Child Welfare Division Director said I should spend at least one night at the Roman Nose State Park which had a lodge. The park is between Oklahoma City and Enid.

I didn't dare say no to my new boss, so I spent a night there on my way to Enid. I had my Conoco credit card to pay for the one night lodging as I sure didn't have much cash at the time. The only

Right Place, Right Time

recollection I now have about my stay at the lodge was its isolation. This was also my first experience staying in a lodge.

At the time I graduated, there were few Indians in the field of social work, and I believe I was hired mainly to work with the Indian populations of Oklahoma. I didn't dare admit to my new employer that at one time I didn't know there were any Indians in Oklahoma. That's what I thought as a youngster when we spent the summer near Stratford.

The first district office to which I was assigned served several counties which had sizeable tribal populations, mostly the Cheyenne and Arapaho. Later I was assigned to another district office that was located in Muskogee that served the Cherokees. At the time, there were only a few Native Americans who had Master degrees in Social Work working in Oklahoma.

In Enid I ended up in an apartment building that was located across the street from the Blue Note Tavern. After I moved into my apartment I didn't want to spend what few dollars I had to purchase housekeeping supplies, so I tried borrowing my neighbor's broom and dust pan the first weekend. Since he wouldn't loan them to me, I had to purchase my own along with other housekeeping essentials. I should mention that I was only going to get paid once a month and I had not received my first check by the time I got to Enid.

After Pat and I married the following year, we moved into a little larger apartment in the same building, and our window faced the Blue Note. We were never able to completely shut out its music and neon lights. Moving into this larger apartment introduced us to the Murphy bed, a bed that is stored standing upright in the wall and pulled down for use, in this instance, in the living room. I believe it was Yogi Berra who was quoted as asking when he was shown a Murphy bed in his hotel room, "What am I supposed to do, sleep standing up?"

Chapter 11 Summer of Transition

After about a month on the job, I went home to return Evelyn's car. I now had to use my old car that blew smoke out of the exhaust pipe every time I pressed on the accelerator as a trade-in. Edna and Francis went with me to Albuquerque to buy a used car. We went to a car lot someplace on Lomas, NE.

In assessing the worth of my car, the car salesman stepped on the gas, and my trade-in responded by blowing out a cloud of smoke. Added to this embarrassment, the car also rocked! Francis and I happened to be standing by the tail pipe when all that smoke blew out on us. The salesman commented about the rocking and the black smoke, to which Francis replied that the car "had a lot of power". I was lucky they took my car as a trade in for a used Beetle, a Volkswagen. After we left the car lot, we couldn't stop laughing about Francis' comment about the power the car supposedly had after I barely got it to the car lot.

Edna gathered some basic kitchen ware for me, including a few recipes, to take back to Enid. She was known for her delicious macaroni and cheese, and she gave me her recipe. When I got back, I tried it out. My pot overflowed with macaroni as I didn't know that macaroni expanded when cooked. It spooked me enough that I didn't try the recipe again. I should have gotten into a boarding house where my meals would be prepared. My cooking, by the way, has never gone beyond fixing chili stew and beans.

Right Place, Right Time

Social Work Career Begins in Oklahoma
Google Images   5/17/14

Chapter 12
Introduction to Social Work - 1962

My First Job

My first full time employment paid $275.00 per month. This had to be my net pay as that's the figure I remember when Pat and I got married in May, 1963. However, this was the most money I had ever earned. Poor Pat at times had to leave grocery items behind at the checkout counter because she didn't have enough to pay for what she was going to buy. At the time our hand-held calculator was a metal pad that had columns of numbers that you could move up and down the pad for adding, using a stylus. The "fancy" digital calculators came much later.

We didn't have much money left by the end of the month. Many times that first summer we used the last few dollars to buy worms for fishing at a nearby lake. It was a struggle to make the money stretch, but I was always confident there would be better days ahead. In fact, at the time I had no idea how great our future was to become.

I enjoyed my introduction to the field of social work as a child welfare worker in this district office. The closest community I worked in was at least fifty miles away, and the job involved a lot of travel, most of the time requiring overnight stays. My caseload consisted of the typical child welfare cases. I did foster and adoptive home studies, placed children in foster homes, and worked with families in their own homes. For the first time I became aware of family breakdowns that I had not been aware of growing up in Guishsche.

This first job was a real eye opener for me. It made me realize that working with individuals and families took a great deal of skill that could only come with experience and professional training.

Right Place, Right Time

This first assignment really helped me in getting a sense of what I needed to learn in order to provide the quality of services that would benefit my clients.

Most of the office staff were longtime residents of the Enid area. Each of them came into social work from differing backgrounds and experiences, so I was really the least experienced of the staff. They were all older than I was, and they were really a good group of people to work with. They were always helpful and encouraging, and I enjoyed working with them. I was glad I ended up in this particular office for my first job, the right place, the right time.

On to More Schooling - 1963

During my first year of employment, I begin thinking about furthering my education in social work. With encouragement from my district office supervisor and others, I decided to apply for admission to a graduate school to work on a Master of Social Work degree. I should add that the state's child welfare director was particularly sensitive to and attempted to provide a viable program of services to the State's Indian population, so I had that office's support for my further training.

The State of Oklahoma had a continuing education program for its social workers. This program paid the tuition and fees for two years of graduate work while keeping the student on its payroll. The commitment was to return to Oklahoma after completing the first year of graduate school, work one year, then return to school for the second year. I don't remember what the commitment was after receiving the graduate degree.

I could not pass up this opportunity. With Pat's help, I applied to two graduate schools I knew had good reputations in social work education. They were the University of Denver Graduate School Of Social Work and the George Warren Brown School of Social Work at Washington University in St. Louis. I couldn't believe I

Chapter 12 Introduction to Social Work

was accepted by both of them as both were and still are top ranked schools of social work. Denver did accept me on a probationary basis.

I chose the University of Denver based strictly on the fact that my younger brother, Walter, and his family were living in Denver at the time. I've never regretted my choice of this school. While the school was unable to confirm it,[23] I believe I was only the second Native American to have graduated from its school of social work up to that time, which was June, 1966. A Navajo student was the first.

GRADUATE SCHOOL OF SOCIAL WORK

In September of 1963, Pat and I left Enid for Denver. We loaded our meager belongings into the smallest U-Haul trailer and pulled it with our VW. In Southeastern Colorado where the elevation begins to rise, we were barely able to pull it over the rolling hills. A Colorado Highway Patrolman told us to pull off to the side of the highway to let the backed up traffic pass. I imagine Pat really began to wonder what she had gotten herself into by marrying me. Remember earlier I told of how I always had to make sure I parked my car on an incline in order for it to roll backwards since the reverse gear didn't work.

I did well in my studies so I was able to get off probation. All I did was study and write papers. What was different from my undergraduate days was that most of my studying had to be done in the university library because of all the research that was required. I learned a lot, and I really enjoyed my course work. I still wasn't good at participating in class, but I got by and got good grades

Right Place, Right Time

Graduate education in social work required both classroom and supervised field work in a social services agency. In my first year, my placement was at the Denver Chapter of the American Red Cross for two days a week. In my second year I was placed at the National Jewish Hospital for two and a half or three days a week. I had classes the remaining days of the week.

We lived close enough to the university that I would walk home for lunch, and then return to the library for more work. In fact on Friday, November 22, 1963 Pat and I were eating lunch while watching TV when the program we were watching was interrupted by the news bulletin that President Kennedy had been shot. Like everyone else, we remained glued to the TV for the rest of the day and days after.

Living in Denver gave me an opportunity to spend time with my brother, Walter. We had not seen much of each other since Ganado. The time in Denver provided both of us the opportunity to interact with each other as adults. Pat and I played cards with Walter and Lena on the weekends, and we babysat their first son, Aaron. Another one of my decisions, to come to Denver, turned out extremely well. I was able to be close to Walter, I got to attend an outstanding graduate school of social work, and Denver was a great place to live.

Return to Oklahoma – Summer, 1964

After completing my first year in June, I returned to work in a district office located in Muskogee. Oh, it was hot and humid in Eastern Oklahoma. Since I had been assigned to work in Cherokee County in Northeastern Oklahoma, we wanted to live in Tahlequah where a state college is located. Pat would be able to complete her final year of college there.

After searching for most of one day for a place to live, we thought we finally found one. We were shown a garage apartment

Chapter 12 Introduction to Social Work

which was literally a dump. We were so discouraged by then that we just drove on to Muskogee, less than thirty miles away, and found an apartment.

Pat had been used to living in hot and humid eastern Oklahoma as she had grown up in the Webbers Falls area near Muskogee, and of course lived in Tulsa. I had somewhat gotten used to it living in Tulsa. When we had gotten to Tahlequah we couldn't believe how miserable it was, even for Pat. We had definitely gotten spoiled with Denver's dry climate.

I enjoyed my work as a child welfare caseworker, mainly working with the Cherokees in Cherokee County. The countryside was beautiful, with tree-covered hills and lots of water. However, I never really adjusted to the office run by a long time employee who was not a trained social worker. I wanted a setting that would provide me an opportunity to grow in my new profession through supervision, and I was unable to get what I wanted. There was a trained social worker on staff, who was rarely called upon by the supervisor for his expertise. I thought his background would have benefited our staff tremendously. I did consult with him on the more difficult situations involving my caseload.

It was during the course of the year that I decided I really wanted to work under a trained social worker in order to continue my growth in the profession. I had my doubts that I would get that by remaining with the state, although my experience in the Enid office had been excellent. There, my supervisor was experienced and was professionally trained, and her staff had been particularly helpful to me.

Once I came to that decision, Pat and I began looking at our options. Pat was about to finish up her senior year at Northeastern in Tahlequah. She had been commuting with several students from Muskogee. Getting her Bachelor of Arts degree increased our confidence about leaving my employment and applying for a stipend

Right Place, Right Time

for my second year of graduate work. I was anxious to leave this district office as soon as my one year obligation ended in June.

We had become active in the local Presbyterian Church. We liked the minister, especially his approachability and the leadership he provided, getting his congregation involved in every day issues of the community and beyond. It was through this church that we decided to do volunteer work for the summer at a small Presbyterian church serving the Mesquakie Indian Settlement in Tama, Iowa. We planned to return to Denver in September. By the time we left my employment in Muskogee, I had been approved for a stipend for my second year from the U. S. Department of Vocational Rehabilitation. This stipend covered my tuition, books and fees, and a living allowance. The obligation was to work a year in a rehabilitation setting upon graduation.

The decision to resign from my position wasn't scary because of my increased self-confidence. The success I had during my first year of graduate school led me to believe that I had gotten into the right line of work, and that I had the potential to become a skilled social worker.

The fact that I had done well with my coursework and had gotten good grades in my field practicum really gave me a major boost. I was able to compete with students who were already practicing social work, who had returned to school, just like I did, to better themselves in the field. I think this was the first time I really felt that I was on my way to being able to compete with anybody, which I hadn't been so sure about up to this point.

Pat's confidence in me added to how I felt about myself. As we left Muskogee for Tama, Iowa, in June, 1965, I was pretty sure I was going to get my graduate degree and get a job in social work after completing my second year of study. On the way to Tama, we stopped in Kansas City to see a Kansas City Athletics baseball game. On our way to the stadium we went the wrong way on a one way

Chapter 12 Introduction to Social Work

street, and to top it off, it was during rush hour. As we came up on top of a high viaduct we got faced with a wall of traffic. Fortunately, I didn't hear anyone yell at us to tell us that we were in the city now, like a driver told me and my friends from Emporia on an earlier visit to Kansas City.

Tama, Iowa, Summer, 1965

Pat and I lived with the minister and his family. The church must have been located right next to the Mesquakie Indian Settlement. This tribe actually purchased the land themselves, rather than the government setting aside the land for them. Despite their private ownership of this land, the tribe eventually began receiving services from the Bureau of Indian Affairs.

Our work with the young people was directed toward getting them involved in constructive activities through the church that included recreational activities. However, most of the students worked for farmers in the area "de-tasselling" corn. I never did learn what this was all about, and we were not particularly busy. It was a small tribe, and we got to know many of the people, although only a few families actually took part in the church's activities.

At the end of the summer, on our way back to Denver, we stopped to attend a church conference at Lake Andes in eastern South Dakota. From there we drove to Rapid City, South Dakota to visit my sister Kathryn and her family. Her husband was stationed at Ellsworth Air Force Base at the time. At the conference we met an Alaskan Native minister who had just begun work with the Department of Indian Work of the Minnesota Council of Churches in Minneapolis. Two years later he talked me into moving to Minneapolis to work for an Indian organization on whose board he sat.

At this conference we also met the late Wendell Chino, who eventually became the long term President of the Mescalero Apache

Right Place, Right Time

Tribe. Mr. Chino was then a minister of a local church in Mescalero, and he was the guest speaker at this conference. He was already an impressive speaker at the time. Many years later as a Bureau of Indian Affairs social worker I became answerable to him when I dealt with his tribe's social services program.

The work we did at Tama was difficult from the standpoint of working with young people who saw our summer program as just something to do. We saw the difficulties confronting the minister in his efforts to serve the community through the church. We also observed the differences in approaches ministers took in serving their congregations. Overall I don't think we had any regrets about how we spent the summer working at this small Presbyterian Church.

Back to Graduate School, 1965

My second year of graduate study was more intense and stressful. It was a busy year of study, writing papers, and spending more time practicing under supervision at the National Jewish Hospital. In addition, my second year involved working on a group research project for our thesis. I completed my graduate education by taking and passing the oral exams.

Pat and I enjoyed the two years we lived in Denver. While I devoted most of my time to my studies, we took time to explore the Denver area, the mountains, the Air Force Academy, and we especially enjoyed the climate.

Pat worked part-time off and on during the two years, including working in a department store during the Christmas holidays when we remained in Denver. My brother, Daniel, and his wife, Rachel came to visit us once. We spent the entire weekend playing cards, only taking a break to see a James Bond movie.

On one of my winter breaks, we drove to Tulsa to visit Pat's family. On the return trip, we got stuck in Dodge City, Kansas for a

Chapter 12 Introduction to Social Work

couple of days due to a fierce snow storm. We were also able to visit my family during my school breaks.

Actually, my two years in graduate school went by fairly quickly, and the break of one year was good for me as it gave me time to try out what I was learning in school. It also helped me to identify areas that I needed to concentrate on in my studies.

During the time I was going to school in Tulsa and Denver, I had been getting a deferment from the military. While in Tulsa I went down to Oklahoma City with a bus load of other future recruits to take my physical. The Viet Nam War was still on by the time I was ready to graduate from Denver, and I anticipated being drafted immediately upon my graduation.

I took an exam for officers training to go in as a social worker; however, I did not pass the exam. I don't remember whether it had to do with early signs of diabetes, or that I was just not officer material. For sure, I was positive that I was going to be drafted, so I had not searched that hard for employment. After I did not get my draft notice, I began my desperate search for a job.

Several of my sisters came to my graduation as I actually took part in the commencement exercises. However, by the evening of my graduation, I was on a train headed to Iowa City, Iowa to interview for a medical social worker position at the University of Iowa Hospitals. If you recall my arrival times at Emporia, Kansas and Tulsa, Oklahoma, I again arrived in Iowa City soon after dawn. I almost fell over when I ran into a schoolmate from Denver in the Iowa City train depot upon my arrival. He was on his way back to his home in Michigan.

Right Place, Right Time

I was interviewed by the hospitals' Social Work Department Director and one of the supervisors. They evidently thought well enough of my background to offer me a Medical Social Worker position.

Upon my return to Denver, Pat and I began packing, again. When it was time to make the final rent payment, the landlady would not accept it, a graduation gift she said. A beautiful ending to our stay in Denver.

Google
Medicine.uiowa.edu
4/5/15

Chapter 13
Social Work - The Right Choice

Move to Iowa City, Iowa

We had purchased a new car just before my graduation, and we looked forward to a safe and problem-free trip to my first big social work job. Guess what? Our new car broke down on the edge of Des Moines, Iowa, on a Saturday evening, and I was to start on my job the following Monday. We were fortunate that we were at a gas station. The fan had come off.

Pat and I spent an uncomfortable night in the car, and the following day we walked to the closest motel which was at least a mile away. The credit card Mr. Garten had given me came in handy. On Monday morning we had the car towed into the car dealership for repairs, and we finally arrived in Iowa City that evening.

We ended up in an unfurnished apartment, and we immediately began looking for more permanent housing as we were expecting our first child in November. It seemed like we had just gotten to Iowa City when my brother Daniel and his wife, Rachel, stopped off to visit us on their way to Washington, D. C. for Dan's new job as a ivil engineer with the Veterans Administration. We went on a picnic in the local park, and I locked my keys in the car. I have a feeling Dan and Rachel were ready to leave when they did. We were able to move into a duplex rather quickly, which was much more comfortable for us as we did not like living in a large apartment complex. Anyway, I thought we were settled, but we were on our way out of Iowa City one year later.

The University of Iowa Hospitals

I reported to work immediately after we finally arrived in Iowa City. I was assigned to work in the rehabilitation unit. I was part of a team made up of the Unit's medical director, the head

Right Place, Right Time

nurse, physical and occupational therapists, and other disciplines that served patients requiring physical rehabilitation services, such as para and quadriplegics.

My work involved providing counseling services to the patients and working with the medical staff in dealing with the patients' social work-related issues. I also coordinated our services with local social work and health agencies throughout Iowa in planning for the return of the patients to their local communities.

I learned a lot working in this setting as my graduate studies began to make sense, and the team really functioned as a team, each one of us contributing our expertise for the benefit of the patients. The Social Work Director was an excellent teaching supervisor. For starters in my new profession, I was again fortunate to have ended up here. Ending up in situations that turned out like they were well planned was becoming a pattern in my journey.

I also had an opportunity to teach an evening class at a local Catholic school of nursing. This was my first experience in teaching. I was able to manage the class fairly well, due to the subject matter being on the family. This course was for the incoming class of new students, which eased my entry into teaching. We had a good semester. I learned a lot, and hopefully the students did too.

Working at the University of Iowa Hospitals provided me an opportunity to observe and to participate in a highly "professional" setting. Because it was a teaching hospital and one that served the people of Iowa state-wide, I got to learn a lot about the people of Iowa, as well as about the state itself. I worked with a highly trained medical staff, including Interns and Residents, and other professionals who were a part of this teaching hospital. I really liked working in this setting, particularly with my social work colleagues.

Living in Iowa City and being associated with the university provided me a chance to attend several of the university's Big Ten Conference football games, a Conference I had only read about. At

Chapter 13 Social Work – The Right Choice

the time, Ed Podolak, who went on to play professional football for the Kansas City Chiefs, was the Hawkeye quarterback. I had access to the University's beautiful championship golf course for a green fee of about $3.00. I had been introduced to golf by some classmates in Denver, and I had only played once or twice before playing on this course. I left behind all the marks of an inept golfer on this beautiful golf course.

The most exciting event was the birth of our son, Brian, who was born in the University of Iowa hospitals in November. His arrival made our stay in Iowa City a most memorable year with all the good things happening to us.

One of my goals when I began my job was to earn my professional certification. The Academy of Certified Social Workers, our professional organization, required two years of supervised work under a professional social worker. So initially my intent was to remain with the Hospitals for at least two years, giving me time to earn this certification, at the same time paying off my obligation of working in a rehabilitation setting.

However, toward the end of my first year in Iowa City, the Alaskan Native minister friend contacted me and offered me the Assistant Director position for the Indian organization he was associated with in Minneapolis. He must have been persuasive as I accepted his offer.

While I really enjoyed my work with the University Hospitals, my long term interests were to work with Indians. At the time I didn't know what kind of social work settings were available that served them. I did know that the Bureau of Indian Affairs had a social services program, but I'm glad I didn't pursue employment with them at this stage of my social work career. So this offer from Minneapolis opened the door for me to enter an area of work I wanted to get into.

Right Place, Right Time

Move to Minneapolis, Minnesota

As I look back on this decision to accept this job offer, it was pretty risky. We had never been to Minneapolis; we didn't know anything about the city nor about the tribes that resided in the area. I knew very little about the Upper Midwest American Indian Center, Inc. I didn't know its source of funding or its stability as an organization. However, as soon as my one year commitment to working in a rehabilitation setting was up in June, 1967, we headed for Minneapolis, Minnesota. We had no idea what the future held for Pat, our infant son, Brian, and me.

Exciting Years at Upper Midwest Indian Center

The Indian Center had existed primarily as a gathering place for the Indian population of Minneapolis and St. Paul, providing limited aid to their fellow citizens. The Center also served as a place where they could continue their traditional and cultural practices.

The Twin Cities was home to many different tribal groups, most of them coming from reservations in the upper Midwest states, such as the Dakotas, Minnesota, Wisconsin, Michigan, Iowa, and at least one from a New Mexico reservation, me. I don't even remember what the organization's source of funding was at the time I was hired. I assume it received some type of a grant as it was now able to hire some staff.

The Center had their offices in a Settlement House in north Minneapolis. A few days into my job I heard this loud female voice from the front part of the building followed by her laughter, saying something to the effect that she had come to meet the "Pueblo." The voice belonged to Ada Deer, a Menominee, who eventually led her tribe to their restoration as a tribe, as well as becoming their tribal Chairperson.

Later Ada, a Columbia University social work graduate, became the Assistant Secretary – Indian Affairs, Department of

Chapter 13 Social Work – The Right Choice

Interior. This first meeting was the beginning of our friendship and our working together on various projects. This included training potential Native American Peace Corps volunteers.

I stayed with the Center for less than a year as the Executive Director and I differed philosophically in our administrative approaches to running the organization. I left and worked temporarily for the Minneapolis Health Department as a social work consultant, then with the Minneapolis Public Schools as a school social worker. After I left my employment with the Center I remained active with the organization as a member of its Board of Directors, eventually serving as its Chairman.

In early 1969, the local Community Health and Welfare Council of Hennepin County, Inc., a social services planning agency, established the American Indian Centers Committee. The committee's task was two-fold. The first task was to study and gain an understanding of the Indian center operations that existed in Minneapolis. The second was to provide this Council with recommendations on how the centers could strengthen their services to their community.[24] This committee was made up of Indians involved in providing services to their community

I happened to be selected to serve on this Committee. Seven organizations identified as "Indian Centers" were selected for the study; one of them was the Upper Midwest American Indian Center. At the completion of the study, the Committee's recommendations were accepted by the Council. The Council in turn submitted them to the United Fund of Minneapolis Area to consider providing financial support for the Center that was selected. As it turned out, Upper Midwest was selected.

| Right Place, Right Time

Robert Carr to Head New Indian Center

TRIBUNE 5-30-69

Robert Carr has resigned as president of the board of the Upper Midwest American Indian Center to become director of a new comprehensive Indian center that is being financed initially by the United Fund of Minneapolis Area.

Carr's resignation was accepted by Upper Midwest's board late Wednesday. The new center is being establIsihed under Upper Midwest's auspices, at the United Fund's request.

Omar Schmidt, executive director of the Community Health and Welfare Council, said pledges of support from three primary sources are being redeemed now.

HE DECLINED to say how much money is being collected, but he said it will be enough to hire a director and a secretary as well as to provide equipment, supplies and utilities. He indicated that funds for programs and "program people" also would be available.

The money raised now is intended to finance the new center through December. By that time, it is anticipated, the center will be a United Fund member and will be able to share in the money raised during next fall's fund drive.

CARR, 28, is a social worker at Phillips Junior High School. He graduated in 1963 with a B.A. degree in sociology from the University of Tulsa, Tulsa, Okla. He earned a master's degree in social work from the University of Denver, Denver, Colo., in 1967.

New chairman of the Upper Midwest board is Bernard J. Bear, a product engineer at Honeywell, Inc. Other new officers are Emile Peake, vice-chairman; Margaret Smith, secretary, and Ed Jefferson, treasurer.

Article from the Minneapolis Tribune Dated May 30, 1969

Chapter 13 Social Work – The Right Choice

The Center's Board was to hire a qualified staff. It was to establish the Indian Center on a solid base so it could undertake the development of a program to meet, as nearly as possible, the needs of the Indian people of all ages living in Minneapolis. After its selection, I resigned from the Board as I was selected as its Executive Director in mid-1969 to undertake this major project. The executive director under whom I had worked when I was first hired by the Center had left the organization by this time.

To initiate these tasks, Upper Midwest was awarded a planning grant for the remainder of the year. It was expected that it would become a United Fund agency the following calendar year, which it became. Approximately $75,000 was awarded to the Center to hire a director and a secretary and to purchase some equipment and supplies.

Fortunately, a most capable secretary was hired. She was efficient, organized, and she took dictation using shorthand. All of what I dictated to her was returned in final form. I tried telling myself that I was really good at dictating, my first experience with this exercise. Rather quickly I had to admit that it was the secretary who was so good in taking dictation and editing my work.

We began our work in a storefront office in south Minneapolis. We eventually moved back to the near north side of the city into larger offices which the organization eventually purchased.

The United Fund and the Health and Welfare Council made available all their professional resources to get us started. They helped us establish the financial records and taught us how to maintain them. The United Fund's public relations section, headed by a Turtle Mountain Chippewa, assisted us with increasing our exposure to the greater Twin Cities area.

I took full advantage of their assistance as their undertaking of this study and then providing the resources to help correct the

Right Place, Right Time

identified gaps in services was really quite historic. Unlike too many established organizations, these two agencies trusted us to take the lead in addressing the findings ourselves.

I particularly recall being invited to speak to one of these two bodies soon after I became the executive director. After my presentation in which I expressed appreciation of our selection to undertake this important endeavor, one of their staff members came up to me afterwards and said, "Don't be so humble."

I don't think the person really appreciated the fact that our community had rarely been trusted to undertake a major task such as the Community Health and Welfare Council and the United Fund had given us. For this opportunity, I only expressed what I had been taught: To always acknowledge and express appreciation for whatever is given to us. Dawaeh, maameh skrowanaama, thank you, we are most appreciative.

These two organizations received criticism from other groups, namely the American Indian Movement, for selecting Upper Midwest. They claimed the organization was "too conservative" and was not representative of the Indian community. Our Board of Directors did consist of a majority of Indians, as required in its by-laws, but we also had members who represented the broader community. The by-laws also required that only Indian members were eligible to hold office on the Board. This broad representation was particularly helpful as the members possessed the backgrounds that were needed to guide its staff in this new venture.

Most of the Board members had long histories of being involved in trying to bring about services to the Indian community. It was also helpful that some of the board members, the non-Indians in particular, were members of organizations with whom we would be working in addressing the community's service needs.

Chapter 13   Social Work – The Right Choice

The Indian members of the Board were longtime residents in the Twin Cities. In addition to their involvement in trying to bring about services to their community, they were familiar with the local issues. This was extremely helpful to a newcomer like me. All in all, I had no problem with the make-up of our Board. Their combined backgrounds and talents, along with those of the staff, made our Center a most viable organization.

Working for this organization for approximately four years is the highlight of my social work career as an administrator. With the help of additional funds for program staff from the United Fund, we began by strengthening the Center's information and referral services for Native people searching for assistance.

At the same time, we began developing an administrative structure with the help of the United Fund. St. Paul already had a Center that served its Native population, so our services focused on the Minneapolis community. We did coordinate our services as there was always movement of Native people between the two cities.

Our organization began growing immediately, both in terms of personnel and programming. By the end of calendar year, 1971,

Right Place, Right Time

according to a report I prepared for a local newsletter, *North Side Pilot,* our Center was operating nine different programs.

In addition to the basic information and referral services, the staff provided an in and after school program for Indian students attending several inner city elementary schools; we operated a halfway house that was managed by a certified alcoholism counselor for newly discharged men from the Work House, the local detention facility; we had a small scholarship program which we named after Dr. Martin Luther King, Jr., that was supported by donations; and we established an adult basic education program. We leased two housing units from the Minneapolis Housing Authority to house newcomers to the cities until permanent housing could be found.

In addition to our funding from the United Fund, some of these programs were supported by contracts with the Minneapolis Public Schools and the Minnesota Governor's Commission on Crime Prevention and Control. Seeking additional funds from other sources was part of our Center's agreement with the United Fund. The Minneapolis Public Schools Board of Education became one of our Center's strong supporters by contracting with us and by allowing our staff to become involved with its efforts in educating Indian children and keeping them in school.

In our efforts to better serve the newcomers to the Twin Cities, we worked actively with and received a great deal of support and cooperation from the local, state, and tribal officials, the state legislators, and the Minneapolis Board of Education. We of course did not provide all the needed services. However, as we coordinated our efforts with the leadership of the other groups, we were able to help the public officials identify and channel additional services and resources to our communities in the Twin Cities.

One of our bigger projects was the Model Urban Indian Center Project. Upper Midwest was selected to be part of a demonstration project involving three other urban Indian centers

Chapter 13 Social Work – The Right Choice

located in Gallup, New Mexico; Los Angeles, California; and Fairbanks, Alaska. This project aimed at consolidating funds from the federal departments, mainly the U. S. Departments of Labor and the Health, Education, and Welfare, now the Department of Health and Human Services. The Bureau of Indian Affairs declined to participate. Its regulations prevented its participation either because our organizations were located in cities, or the services were directed to those who were no longer residing on their reservations.

The overall goal of this project was to develop comprehensive and coordinated services to Indians residing in these cities through joint funding by the federal agencies. I was part of a team that traveled to these locations, accompanied by a professional writer, to develop the proposal seeking these funds. The project was funded, and its implementation began in 1971.

All these programs were carried out by a staff of thirty eight people, according to my report. Our staff, practically all of them Native Americans, consisted of a mixture of young and older adults, and they were a most capable staff. Two of the younger staff members eventually entered graduate schools of social work and became professional social workers. One went on to law school and later worked in the State Attorney General's office. One of the Indian board members eventually entered and graduated from Harvard.

The elders, both staff and volunteers, provided us counsel about the traditions of their people. They also served as reminders that we were more than just a typical service organization. Whatever we did, we needed to serve the community according to what we determined to be effective. How we served our community did not necessarily have to be the way the established agencies expected us to do things.

I benefited tremendously from all these people, and together we built a dynamic and viable organization of services. It

Right Place, Right Time

was, I believe, the first Indian organization to offer a broad spectrum of services in the Twin Cities. By the time I left, the organization's budget was over $300,000, a budget that had grown from the initial grant of $75,000 from the United Fund.

My employment at Upper Midwest also coincided with the beginnings of the federal Office of Economic Opportunity's War on Poverty efforts. As a result of President Lyndon Johnson's Great Society legislative agenda, the Office of Economic Opportunity, OEO, was created, and federal dollars began coming into community-based organizations. This office created such programs as VISTA, Volunteers in Service to America, the Job Corps, Head Start, and the Community Action Programs. This federal agency focused its efforts on getting greater participation of poor people, especially the minorities, in decision-making affecting their communities and becoming the actual providers of services to their communities.

This opportunity for our involvement required us to attend meeting after meeting, day after day and what seemed like night after night. Most of these meetings involved heated discussions among the representatives of the various communities and organizations about services, and who should, or shouldn't get funds. I have never attended so many meetings before or after my Minneapolis days. Because program administrators and residents were going to be affected by decisions made in these meetings that involved policies, funds, and services, we couldn't afford to not attend these meetings.

Some of you may recall slogans of those days, such as "maximum feasible participation" and "power to the people." These two slogans were very descriptive of what took place in Minneapolis. It was exciting to see the impact the Office of Economic Opportunity had locally and to be a part of it.

The American Indian Movement, in particular, gained traction during this period. Its early leaders, such as Dennis Banks

Chapter 13   Social Work – The Right Choice

and Clyde Bellecourt, had their beginnings and headquarters in Minneapolis. Our two organizations differed on how to address the efforts of self-determination, and these differences exposed the divisions within our community. The American Indian Movement was the more outspoken and aggressive advocate of Indian rights. There were those of the more moderate persuasion, such as Upper Midwest, who had similar values and goals, mainly differing on the approaches to reaching them.

There was the usual name calling that went on in our community, such as some being referred to as "Apples", white on the inside and red on the outside. In fact, there was a suburb where a number of Indians lived that was referred to as Apple Valley.

I and others were confronted by questions about our "Indianness": whether we could still be Indians if we possessed formal training, held responsible positions, worked with the non-Indian community, or lived outside the inner city. Do we become less Indian when we do not participate in traditional practices, particularly the ceremonial practices? These are questions that still persist today, but maybe not at the level that existed when we first began to truly engage in our self-determination efforts.

Despite these differences and our many heated disagreements, the Upper Midwest's services and AIM's more vocal and aggressive approach to advocating our rights, broadened our impact. The greater community also became more aware of the needs and goals of its native population. As a result a large segment of the community became involved in working with us.

Thinking back to all that transpired during this time, it was really quite impressive how the people and institutions of the greater Twin Cities, including the state legislators, and some of the state's tribal officials, responded to our efforts when they were given the opportunity. While it may not have always been this way in the past, I found their responses to be quite exemplary.

Right Place, Right Time

Opportunities for involvement with social and political issues and services were numerous. My position with the Center led to my participation in various task forces, committees, and work groups locally, regionally, and nationally. My participation allowed me to provide input on what I had learned about social work and organizational matters involving Native Americans.

I had the opportunity to testify before a congressional committee on Indian education. During this particular hearing, members of the congressional committee would get up and leave, then return, during the testimonies. I thought that was pretty disrespectful to those of us who were testifying, until I learned later that they had to leave to vote and that all the testimonies were recorded. I was pretty naïve then.

Another exciting experience that I never expected to have was my involvement with the preparation of President Richard Nixon's *Address to the United States Congress* on Indian self-determination which he gave on July 8, 1970. The White House Aide who worked with our small group was Brad Patterson, executive assistant to Leonard Garment. Mr. Garment was President Nixon's Special Counsel. These two men were credited with being primarily responsible for drafting this speech, which was a message on the establishment of tribal self-determination as a basic federal policy.

I didn't realize it at the time, but this was a critically important speech as it initiated a major shift in the federal government's relationship with Native Americans. I had this opportunity to participate because I was involved in the development of the demonstration project for the multi- agency funding, one of the efforts to enhance our self-determination. My group's efforts resulted in a few lines in the speech we worked on in the Old Executive Office Building in Washington. We were never introduced to the President.

Chapter 13 Social Work – The Right Choice

Helped write this speech

FOR RELEASE AT 12:00 NOON, EDT　　　　　　　　　July 8, 1970

Office of the White House Press Secretary

- -

THE WHITE HOUSE

TO THE CONGRESS OF THE UNITED STATES:

　　The first Americans -- the Indians -- are the most deprived and most isolated minority group in our nation. On virtually every scale of measurement -- employment, income, education, health -- the condition of the Indian people ranks at the bottom.

　　This condition is the heritage of centuries of injustice. From the time of their first contact with European settlers, the American Indians have been oppressed and brutalized, deprived of their ancestral lands and denied the opportunity to control their own destiny. Even the Federal programs which are intended to meet their needs have frequently proven to be ineffective and demeaning.

11

will get better programs and that public monies will be more effectively expended if the people who are most affected by these programs are responsible for operating them.

　　The Indians of America need Federal assistance -- this much has long been clear. What has not always been clear, however, is that the Federal government needs Indian energies and Indian leadership if its assistance is to be effective in improving the conditions of Indian life. It is a new and balanced relationship between the United States government and the first Americans that is at the heart of our approach to Indian problems. And that is why we now approach these problems with new confidence that they will successfully be overcome.

RICHARD NIXON

THE WHITE HOUSE,

　July 8, 1970.

\# \# \# \#

Helped write this President Nixon's

　　Another exciting adventure was my trip to Puerto Rico to assist with training a group of young Native Americans who were planning to join the Peace Corps. My flight to Puerto Rico was my first commercial airline flight. To make matters worse, this trip took

199

Right Place, Right Time

place during the time something was going on in the airline industry where airline traffic was almost brought to a standstill.

My connecting flight from New York was to leave early evening, but it did not leave until about midnight. I saw long lines of planes waiting to take off as we also waited in line. Like all my previous journeys to new destinations, I again arrived in San Juan, Puerto Rico about dawn. This time my arrival time was not previously planned.

I picked up my travel instructions to the training site at the San Juan airport, which was to catch a "publico" to Arecibo, approximately fifty miles west of San Juan on the northern coast of Puerto Rico. I got there, a little shaky, as this was my first trip outside the continental United States, and I did not speak a word of Spanish. My knowledge of a foreign language was limited to a few words in German, which I learned in my German class at Emporia.

My travel provided me with many exciting and fun experiences. One time I was attending a meeting in New York City, and several of us decided to go to Times Square to look around after the day's meetings were over. We saw on a theatre marquee that a very popular Broadway show was playing. We decided that we wanted to see it so we walked up to the ticket counter and told the young lady that we wanted tickets for the show. She looked at her schedule, and then told us the next available tickets were for some time that fall. I think we were there in the spring of that year.

My move to Minneapolis was another instance of where I ended up being in the right place at the right time. Up to this time, Indians, even those with professional training, were not in great demand for employment by established agencies. Even those, whose programs were directed at us, such as the Bureau of Indian Affairs and the Indian Health Services, seemed resistant to hiring Indians.

Chapter 13 Social Work – The Right Choice

If I had not met the Alaskan Native minister at the church conference in South Dakota, I may have never had the experiences working with the organizations I've talked about. These were organizations that had assumed leadership roles in advocating for the self-determination of all people. These agencies, such as the Community Health and Welfare Council of Hennepin County, Inc., the United Fund, and the Office of Economic Opportunity programs made it possible for organizations, such as Upper Midwest, to decide ways of serving their communities.

Greater Twin Cities United Way

Greater Twin Cities United Way unites caring people to build pathways out of poverty, creating opportunity for all.

1960s: United Ways in Minneapolis and St. Paul responded to ethnic and social transformation by serving more communities of color and low-income individuals.
https://www.gtcuw.org/about_us/history/   11/18/13

These organizations, particularly the Health and Welfare Council and the United Fund, impressed me tremendously for what they did for our Indian community in Minneapolis. I and many others became involved in helping formulate policies and programs that we thought would best work for us. Most of us had not experienced having a voice in determining much about our lives. These organizations provided us the greatest opportunity to become active participants in our self-determination efforts.

I learned a tremendous amount from my experiences in Minneapolis. For many of us who were managing these programs, it was the first time we were in positions of authority and held accountable for being in charge of large sums of money. One of the most important lessons I learned is that as people are trusted and given responsibilities to carry out, like the Health and Welfare

Right Place, Right Time

Council and the United Fund did with us, people tend to flourish and the best comes out of us. I saw this take place at the Upper Midwest American Indian Center as we went about trying to serve our fellow Native Americans in the Twin Cities.

So I've tended to use what I experienced there as a standard when I evaluate how we are served and treated in other parts of the country, and the level of opportunities we are given to decide for ourselves what is best for us. I have very positive memories of the people of the Twin Cities and the State of Minnesota.

Chapter 14
Bureau of Indian Affairs

In 1973, we decided to leave Minneapolis to return to the Southwest. I had previously met two individuals from Laguna Pueblo, who also happened to be from my village, at a conference in Minneapolis. Both of them were employed by the Bureau of Indian Affairs in Albuquerque.

They encouraged me to apply for employment with that agency. In fact, one of them wrote a letter to the agency's supervisory social worker after he returned to his office suggesting she get in touch with me for possible employment. Nobody contacted me. After we got back to New Mexico, I learned about the vacancy involving the Supervisory Social Worker position at the Southern Pueblos Agency in Albuquerque. I immediately submitted my application.

About the time I applied, there were two major events that were about to take place in the Bureau, which I was not aware of at the time of my application. These two events would transform the Bureau in major ways.

The first involved Indian employment preference in the Bureau, which also would affect the Indian Health Service. A class action suit had been filed by a group of non-Indian Bureau

Right Place, Right Time

employees claiming that the Indian employment preference violated the anti-discrimination provisions of the Equal Employment Opportunity Act of 1972. The U. S. District Court for the District of New Mexico agreed. On appeal of this decision by the Secretary of the Interior, the U. S. Supreme Court ruled on June 17, 1974, to uphold the employment preference policy in the Bureau.[25]

The Supreme Court had not yet decided by the time I applied. I got the impression that my hiring was delayed because the agency was waiting to learn whether the Supreme Court was going to uphold Indian preference. There were several non-Indian applicants applying for this position, and all of them were currently employed in the social services department. Even though I had the same educational credentials as the other applicants and more experience in program administration, I doubt very much if I would have been hired given the Bureau's track record.

The second major event was the policy shift that was soon to take place as the result of the passage of P. L. 93-638, *The Indian Self-Determination and Education Assistance Act of 1975*, which would drastically change the Bureau's relationships with the tribal governments. Except for a few functions, this law authorized tribes to enter into contracts with the Bureau to operate its various programs. Its social services program was one that became contractible under this law.

My experiences in Minneapolis had convinced me that we could do as good a job, or better, in managing and providing the services ourselves. I immediately began advocating for the tribes to contract, and before long, a number of them began initiating requests to contract the social services program. Joining the Bureau at this time was perfect timing for me as I got another opportunity to play a role in the Indian self-determination efforts.

These two major shifts in Bureau policies and practices caused a major upheaval among the personnel as most of the

Chapter 14 Bureau of Indian Affairs

supervisory positions were occupied by non-Indians at the time, and these two policies were now going to affect both employment and advancement opportunities for them. Indian preference in employment was already in place before the suit was filed by the non-Indian employees. However, once the U. S. Supreme Court upheld this policy, there was no longer a question about preference for employment in the Bureau.

In addition to the dilemma faced by the non-Indian employees, the implementation of P. L. 93-638 held additional implications for all the employees. As the tribes took over Bureau programs, its personnel had to be reduced as the program administration budget would be transferred to the tribes to operate the contracted programs.

Not only was I faced with this environment brought about by these policy shifts, but my hiring was also controversial. There were rumors to the effect that my Minneapolis experience really did not provide the right kind of experience to manage a Bureau program. My initial actions in this position also caused concerns that I was too aggressive as a supervisor. They were probably right because my prior position in Minneapolis required me to make timely decisions due to the competitive and fast-paced environment in which I worked. I now entered a work environment that in my judgment was slow in decision making and actions.

These were the results of the hierarchy one had to go through to get approval for decisions. In addition, there was also the prevailing attitude that this was the way decisions and actions had always been carried out, and long-time employees seemed to have difficulty breaking away from that mode.

I quickly became convinced that prior experience working in a different type of setting, preferably a private setting, was extremely valuable before joining a bureaucracy. My prior experiences had taught me that generally there are numerous

Right Place, Right Time

options to consider when implementing an agency's mission, an area which I found to be quite restrictive in the Bureau.

This was an area which became somewhat problematic for my superiors and me. My transition from being a part of a community that was trying to get the established bureaucracies to change to becoming a member of such a bureaucracy caused me some adjustment problems, too. So it took a while for my superiors and me to adjust to each other's ways of managing the Bureau functions. I don't think we ever fully succeeded in adjusting to each other's ways of doing things.

Having to deal with policies and operating procedures that had been established decades ago and were still being used, was particularly frustrating. I had been involved in formulating policies and procedures at the Indian Center that were current with the times and were far more applicable than what I found in the Bureau. However, the changing environment in the Bureau did give me opportunities to use the experience I had gained in Minneapolis.

Initially, my job was supervising a staff of four social workers who were providing direct services to the ten southern pueblo tribes. Fairly quickly, my role began changing from overseeing the Bureau services to assisting the contracting tribes to develop policies and procedures, as well as providing basic social work training for the new tribal personnel.

An Area Social Services Staff Meeting

Chapter 14 Bureau of Indian Affairs

I don't know if the Bureau administrators ever accepted the fact that my Minneapolis experience was very useful in the implementation of P. L. 93-638 and the contracting of its social services program.

P. L. 93-638 basically reversed the Bureau's historical role with the tribal governments. The tribes were now going to determine how they were going to be served through their contracted programs. This role reversal at times involved me in controversies having to do with the continued role of the Bureau.

Our major task was to help the tribes establish social services programs that would be capable of meeting needs that ranged from financial assistance to problems of child abuse and neglect. These efforts were oftentimes seen as the Bureau not wanting to let go of its role. I found that people in general have a tendency to view social work as a field that does not necessarily require professional training. They think that as long as you like people and are good to them, these characteristics are basically all that is required to "do social work."

Trying to convince some of the new contractors otherwise sometimes impacted my working relationships with them. These major policy shifts created an environment that the federal agencies were not used to. This had to do with having to let go of their controls over Bureau policies and program decisions that now shifted to the tribal governments. For example, as much as I wanted the tribes to hire trained social services personnel for their contracted programs, it was now a tribal decision. This took some getting used to. Slowly, and perhaps grudgingly, the feds eased up on some of their controls. I guess I should include myself, as I was now a "Fed."

My high expectations for performance caused discomfort for my agency administrators and for the tribes, as well as those whose work I oversaw. This did not seem to be problematic in Minneapolis, but these expectations did affect my working relationships in the

Right Place, Right Time

Bureau. I tend to think that the level of performance was not very high in the Bureau, and some of the tribes too often excused it for its mediocre performance.

Whereas, in Minneapolis the prevailing attitude in the Indian community was that we finally had a chance to do for ourselves, so let's not let this opportunity go to waste. As a result of this attitude, we did great things together. While I should probably only speak for myself, all my siblings exhibit this characteristic of high expectations. I believe we learned this from our parents. As much as I hate to admit it, my parents probably got better results from us than I did in the Bureau.

Another outgrowth of these policy changes, particularly the passage of P. L. 93-638, resulted in the explosion of tribal "consultants," most of whom were not Indian. These "consultants" tended to assume the role of spokespersons for the tribes in dealing with the Bureau. Very often they pitted tribal officials and their personnel against Bureau employees, taking advantage of the conflicting relationships tribes have always had with the Bureau.

Oftentimes it appeared that the "consultants" focused too much on getting the tribes to make immediate and complete breaks from the Bureau. I thought they could have been more helpful to the tribes by advising them to take advantage of the Bureau resources that were still available to them.

I also felt that some of the advice these "consultants" gave the tribes were more of a hindrance to them, keeping the tribes from taking full advantage of the opportunity to determine for themselves what would work. Too often the consultants were determining what was good for the tribes, just like the federal agencies had.

Besides the tribes, these "consultants" became major beneficiaries of P. L. 93-638, by opening up job opportunities for themselves, as well as getting into decision-making positions with

Chapter 14 Bureau of Indian Affairs

the tribes. It took some time for the tribes to begin hiring Indians as consultants. I saw this throughout my employment with the Bureau.

The tribes had a tendency to trust the white men's judgment over those of their own people. While many Native people employed by the Bureau may deny it, this attitude did undermine some of our efforts in working with our own people. Many of the non-Indian employees saw this as proof that tribes preferred to work with them rather than with their fellow Indians.

After leaving the Southern Pueblos Agency, I moved on to the regional offices in Albuquerque as an Area Social Worker, overseeing the Bureau's social services programs in the Albuquerque region which encompassed New Mexico and Colorado. From there I moved to the Bureau's Central Offices in Washington, D. C. as the Deputy Director of Social Services. We didn't like living in the Washington, D. C. area, nor did I like job I had taken.

Luckily the regional social work position in Portland, Oregon opened up. I applied and was selected. So after one year in Washington, we were on our way to Portland. My responsibilities were similar to those I had in the Albuquerque regional office, which was overseeing the office's social services to the tribes in the Pacific Northwest.

In the early 1980's my family vacationed in the Pacific Northwest, and we had gone through Portland. We thought this would be a nice place to live. In May, 1990, we ended up living in this beautiful part of the country and in the great city of Portland.

I got to work with tribes who lived on beautiful forested and seaside reservations in the Pacific Northwest, including one tribe whose reservation is located on the northwestern tip of the Olympic Peninsula, in Washington State. The tribal offices were located right on the shore of the Strait of Juan de Fuca.

We served one tribe in southeastern Alaska, and getting to their island community I had to take a ten minute flight from

Right Place, Right Time

Ketchikan in a small plane that took off and landed on water. I had never seen more than one eagle at any one time. Here, I saw bald eagles everywhere, even right in the midst of this village, just like common birds.

I also remember my first trip to this island community from Portland. My commercial flight was to Ketchikan, Alaska. I did not know I had to catch a ferry to cross a channel from the airport to the town. It was pouring down rain when I arrived, and I called the hotel for their shuttle. After it did not arrive for some time, I called again, and they said they could not find me. That's when I found out I had to catch a ferry, and the driver was waiting for me at the dock on the other side of the channel.

I finally achieved my long time goal of becoming a certified social worker and becoming a member of our professional organization, the Academy of Certified Social Workers. It took me over thirty years to achieve it. Since leaving the University of Iowa Hospitals, I did not have a social worker supervising my work as required by the Academy.

In Portland I worked out an arrangement with a professional social worker to oversee my work so that I could meet the supervisory requirements. I took the written examination and finally received my certification even though it was only a few years before my retirement.

I had previously gone through another experience that related to my quest for professional certification. Just about the time I was leaving Albuquerque in 1989 for the central office, the State of New Mexico issued rules for the licensing of social workers. As I recall, those already possessing the necessary credentials for the different levels of licensure, were "grandfathered" in.

Since I was leaving the state, I never applied for a license. However, for several months after leaving the state, I was writing reference letters for those Bureau social workers in the Albuquerque

Chapter 14 Bureau of Indian Affairs

Area jurisdiction who had applied for licenses. When I returned to New Mexico after my retirement, all these social workers had the highest level social work licenses, while the author of all those reference letters, me, had to take an exam to get an entry level license.

While the Bureau initially wondered whether I had the right kind of experience to manage its social services program, I like to think it did pay off for both of us. As I moved from the agency level to the regional and national offices, my responsibilities shifted from direct services to tribes to policy development.

The two policy shifts I've discussed had resulted in retirements of many of the long-time regional and central office social services program administrators. This resulted in an influx of new social workers such as me, who came from varied social work experiences. This movement initiated a more assertive effort to strengthen and broaden the Bureau's social work program and practices in order to meet the changing societal issues confronting the tribes.

One example was the introduction of a structured orientation program geared to new social services personnel. This was initiated by two regional social workers. I believe one or perhaps both of them came from a teaching background. This turned into a Bureau-wide training program. Up to this time, whatever orientation was provided was at the initiative of the regional personnel and so the quantity and quality varied among regions. Once the central office sanctioned this newly introduced orientation effort, the training became standardized.

I became a part of a network of trainers that held periodic regional training sessions for the Bureau and tribal social services personnel in the areas of administration and program. I thought this was particularly timely in view of new personnel being hired by tribes who had contracted the Bureau's social services programs.

Right Place, Right Time

Another major initiative was the introduction of Bureau-wide social service program reviews in an effort to strengthen the services to tribes. This led to my involvement with my Bureau colleagues in updating the policies and practices of the social services program. I thought the regional social workers I worked with were especially committed to effecting policies that would result in the best possible services.

I also observed the move toward professionalizing and expanding the Bureau's social services program. While often times our work was compromised because we did not have the final authority in many program-related decisions, it did not deter us from trying to improve the ways the people were served.

I enjoyed my work with the Bureau, although my experiences never quite got to the level of excitement that I experienced in Minneapolis. However, the Bureau did provide me with many additional experiences and opportunities.

The downside was that often times important social work-related decisions were made based solely on political considerations by agency administrators. The human services programs, such as Social services, Education, and the Employment Assistance programs also took a back seat to those functions that focused on land, property, natural resources, and trust-related programs in terms of support and funding.

It is also my impression that all too often, the longer one stayed in the Bureau, the more the focus tended to shift from job performance to a focus on promotions, awards, and other benefits offered by the federal government. The annual performance evaluation, which often resulted in monetary awards, was a good example of the weaknesses and inconsistencies of what supervisors viewed as good performance. It seemed easier to hand out awards than to be faced with appeals of their supervisory decisions, or accusations of unfairness.

Chapter 14 Bureau of Indian Affairs

There were also some good supervisors and skilled personnel, so the weaknesses I've mentioned are not true across the board. Most of the people I worked with, besides having the credentials for their positions, also had the best interests of the people they were serving. While there were some professionally-trained Indian employees, not many were in positions of authority at the time, as it is only recently that Indian preference in hiring has become the norm.

I worked for the Bureau until I took early retirement in 1999. I thought it was the right time for me to leave. I did not want to be one of those employees "who never left". As an acquaintance commented to me on my departure, "I didn't think anyone ever left the Bureau." An observation that maybe too many of us overstayed.

I left the Bureau with a sense of accomplishment, and many memories, particularly of my early days in the Bureau. Joining the Bureau was by itself a major change for me as far as the work environment was concerned. I also entered the Bureau at a time when it was being forced to make major policy changes in its relationship with the tribes.

Because these changes forced both the Bureau and the tribes to make major adjustments in how they conducted business with each other, this transition created tension, particularly between the non-Indian and Indian employees. This tension also existed between Bureau employees and the tribal governments simply because the roles they had been so used to playing had been reversed.

Right Place, Right Time

I also have fun memories. For example, one time a colleague asked a tribal official if I shouldn't be invited to a meeting that involved a discussion of some social services issues. His reply, "We can do without Bob Carr." This may sound like a hurtful comment, but when I view it in the context of the changed roles of the Bureau and the tribes, I have to chuckle, as this particular tribal official seemed to have adjusted to this role reversal rather quickly.

My favorite memory was when I showed up at work one day wearing a mismatched, one brown and one black, pair of shoes. It was a day the field staff had come in for a meeting, and whom I was intending to impress, until one of them asked me, "What's with the shoes?"

There were Bureau policies and practices I disagreed with. Despite my discomfort with them, I did enjoy my time with the agency, especially the opportunity to work with some of my colleagues in updating Bureau social services program policies, as well as formulating new ones to support the changes brought about by the passage of P. L. 93-638.

My employment also gave me the opportunity to become familiar with the many tribes across the country. I found out that the Kawaigame mahtra, Lagunas, were not the only tribe in this country as I once thought when my family spent the summer in Oklahoma as a youngster. I may have missed some aspects of life by moving around, both geographically and in work settings. With all that I have experienced, I have no regrets about the route that I traveled. If I had to do it all over again, I would probably do the same thing.

My experiences, without question, have enriched my life and my wife, Pat's, for she later journeyed with me and helped me in getting to the right places at the right times. All this happened because of the people I have talked about in this story.

Reflections on My Journey

Writing about my journey encouraged me to examine more closely how my life evolved, beginning with my childhood. I've thought about how my life has been so affected by individuals, places, and especially the timing of events that propelled me on to many exciting experiences. The timing of these events and where they took place is so amazing to me. It's like a blue-print had been prepared for me to follow. I realize that I could have easily not recognized, nor taken advantage of the opportunities.

Fortunately I had evidently developed some sense of responsibility and self-confidence early on that allowed me to try out new experiences. I had few role models of students going on to college at the time.

Each major segment through which I've traveled, i.e., leaving home, boarding school, college, and employment was made possible by the people I've talked about. They believed I was capable of taking this journey and they stood by me throughout.

So, in addition to my family, there was something very special about the people in my story, i.e., the people of my village, the Ganado Mission faculty and staff, the Garten family, my wife Pat, and many others whom I have not mentioned by name. They are special because they contributed so much to my success, but more importantly, they saw something special in me and acknowledged this in their relationships with me.

Even more special about them is that they would have treated others the same way they treated me. I hope I will surprise them as they read about how much I appreciated them, and how they inspired me.

To all of them, Dawaeh, Gaamamehskrunama. Thank you, I am most grateful.

Wah heh meh. That is all.

Right Place, Right Time

Acknowledgements

After losing our parents, and seeing how all the Carr siblings were leading productive lives, I began to marvel at the impact they had on us. So, I wanted to tell others about them, and the idea about putting it in writing crossed my mind off and on for a number of years before I actually began. My initial thoughts were writing just about my parents. I finally decided that I could better describe their tremendous influences on us by telling about my journey. All that I have accomplished has been the result of their influences.

What finally gave me the impetus to write was when one of the television networks, as a part of its newscast, featured a Black couple of very modest means from the South. Their children grew up to become quite prominent in their chosen fields of work. I thought the family resembled my own family, not necessarily about any of us becoming prominent in our fields. Rather it was more about how both sets of children had flourished because of how our parents raised us.

In 2005, I responded to a solicitation by the former U. S. Senator John Edwards' *One America Committee*, to submit stories about the homes we grew up in, that he would edit for publication. These stories, including mine, were published in *HOME; Blueprints of our Lives*, in November, 2006. I actually saw an excerpt of mine and Danny Glover's story on the *One America Committee* website preceding the publication of the book. I began thinking that I could actually write a book.

For additional practice at writing, I wrote an account of the tour my wife and I took to China in 2009, entitled, *From Mutton to Peking Duck, An Eight Day Glimpse of China*, which is unpublished. After these two experiences in writing, I began working on *Right Place, Right Time; The Journey of a Pueblo of Laguna Native*.

Right Place, Right Time

I want to acknowledge the following individuals for their parts in helping me pull off this story.

Kathryn, Alice, Elgin, Evelyn, and Daniel, my brothers and sisters, each of whom contributed with their stories. While they may have been leery about what I would write, they willingly shared their memories of our parents and relatives, as well as their experiences.

My classmate and friend, Marilyn "Sammie" Watchman Dalton. When I couldn't quite remember something about my days at Ganado, it was Sammie I called upon. Your memory impresses me. You even remembered that I "skated up a storm" on our senior trip. I didn't even remember that I knew how to roller-skate. My thanks for happily sharing what you remembered of our fun school days many years ago.

The volunteer staff at the Menaul Historical Library in Albuquerque for helping me find some of the records on Ganado Mission, including two papers my sister, Kathryn, wrote for her English class.

Mr. Roland Johnson. Your review and suggestions involving my phonetic spelling of our language were extremely meaningful and helpful. Thank you, also, for sharing with me additional background information on the ways of our people, which strengthened my story. Dawaheh, Umu.

Donna McBroom. Your editing has made my story sound even better. I could not have produced this book without your involvement and support. Thank you.

Aaron Carr and Sandra Merriman. For your review of my manuscript and for your helpful comments and suggestions. Thank you, Aaron, for sharing with me the realities of publishing.

My wife, Pat and our two granddaughters, Stephanie and Rhiannon. For your contributions in the preparation of this book. Your involvement has meant a great deal to me.

Afterword

Zeyubado, Pedro Carr. My father died June 10, 1977 at the age of 75. He and my mother were at their sheep camp at Skro kana, where he was still tending his beloved herd of sheep when he began feeling ill. Evelyn told us that dad gave mother very specific instructions just before his passing in an Albuquerque hospital where he had been taken.

Before leaving him to return home to pick up some clothes so she could return to be with him he told her, Dru wah we shats gues kaneeru*, bah truwa beh, Tell the sheep farewell! Our father died within hours of mother's departure from his side where she had been during their fifty one years of marriage. My dad has always served as my role model as a man and as a father.

Zawayduetsa, Edith Pacheco Carr. My mother died July 24, 1995, at the age of eighty nine. She had spent her last decade living in our tribe's assisted living care facility. What she taught me about faith, about how to deal with physical disabilities, and what she did for our family and others have served as standards I've tried striving for, although never quite getting close to reaching them.

My Brothers and Sisters

Kathryn Carr Romero. Her family returned to Guishsche after her husband retired from the military. Upon their return she worked for the tribe in several of their human services programs. Since her retirement she has remained active in senior programs. She is teased for never being at home, but she is our family's model of how we should age. She is also the holder of many Senior Olympic medals. Her home now serves as our gathering place since the passing of our parents. Kathryn has two children, James and Bruce.

Right Place, Right Time

Alice Ethel Carr Ottipoby. Alice lived away from the reservation the longest. After living briefly in Michigan, she and her husband, Collins, moved to Tucson, Arizona. Collins taught at the Tucson Indian Training School, a Presbyterian boarding school. They moved to Kingman, Arizona where they lived until they retired.

Alice had a varied career as a registered nurse. She worked as an Intensive Care nurse and with a team of health professionals who served a tribe in the Supai Canyon in Arizona. The team had to be transported to the bottom of the canyon either on the backs of mules or by helicopter. She worked as a private nurse escorting patients who were being transported by private plane. She also worked with a doctor at the Ford Proving Grounds in Yucca, Arizona. In 2005 she and Collins returned to Guishsche where they currently reside. They have one daughter, Janet.

Edna Lupe Carr Smith. Trained as a secretary/bookkeeper, she worked in those capacities with several organizations, including the Bureau and for our tribe. Edna was the one sibling who remained in the Albuquerque and Laguna area throughout her life. She was an extremely sensitive and caring sister, just like her husband, Francis. They have two adopted daughters, Edith and Margaret. We lost Edna and Francis in a tragic car accident in 1973.

Elgin Earl Carr. Elgin retired from the federal government as an instructor at the Southwestern Indian Polytechnic Institute in Albuquerque, and then continued teaching at the Santa Fe Indian School until he retired from there. After all the fuss he put up about going to school during his childhood, Elgin went on to receive his Bachelor's degree from Eastern New Mexico University. After the death of his wife, Reba, he moved back to Guishsche where he currently resides. He and Reba have three children, Anson, Elgin, and Sadie.

Evelyn Carr Tonkinson. Evelyn graduated from Westminster College and received her Master's degree in Elementary Education

Afterward

from Colorado State College, now University of Northern Colorado. She taught in the Bureau's Elementary Schools at Acoma, Laguna, and Isleta Pueblos until her retirement. She and her husband, David, have one daughter, Pamela. Evelyn currently resides in Albuquerque.

Daniel Carr. After receiving his Civil Engineering degree, he worked for the Veterans Administration in Washington, D. C. He left the Veterans Administration to work for the Corps of Engineers in Albuquerque and Omaha, Nebraska. He returned to Albuquerque to work for the Bureau until he retired. He and his wife Rachel reside in the village of Ha-dzaatya,* Mesita. Daniel served as his village's Tribal Council Representative for a number of years. He also continued his interest in livestock, switching from sheep to the cattle business. He and Rachel have two children, Shannon and Stacey.

Robert Charles Carr. I retired as a social worker in 1999, and Pat and I returned to Albuquerque where we currently reside. Our son, Brian, retired as a Commander from the Albuquerque Police Department. He and his wife, JoAnn Abeyta, have two daughters, Stephanie Ann and Rhiannon Marie.

Walter Jacob Carr. After completing high school he attended Draughons Business College in Albuquerque where he concentrated on accounting. Thereafter, he participated in the Bureau of Indian Affairs Relocation Program, an employment placement program. He and his family resided in Denver, Colorado, eventually returning to Albuquerque where he was employed with the Bureau. Walter and Lena have two sons, Aaron and Kyle. Walter died in a car accident in June, 1985.

The Other Important People in My Life

Patricia Merriman Carr. Pat received her Master's in Library Science from the University of Minnesota. She retired as a high school librarian. Pat is one of the persons who entered my life at a

Right Place, Right Time

critical juncture in my journey, and who has propelled me throughout our marriage. Without her love, encouragement, and support, I would not have undertaken many of the ventures I've described.

Carl and Nola Merriman. My future in-laws fed me when my finances were about depleted. They, like my parents, demonstrated to me that despite limited resources, parents can build strong foundations for their children, just as they did with their three daughters. The Merrimans accepted me into their family during a time when opinions about Indians were not especially good.

The Garten Family. This family provided what I needed to move along on my journey. I could not have found a more loving family than the Gartens. Their home was where I always seemed to regain my equilibrium. I've lost both Mr. and Mrs. Garten and Ted's sister, Nancy. Dr. Ted Garten retired as Professor of Education and Chair of the Curriculum and Instructions Department, Central Missouri State University. Ted and his wife, Mary, reside in Warrensburg, Missouri. They have three children, Kevin, Kirk, and Megan. They remain our dear friends.

My Journey

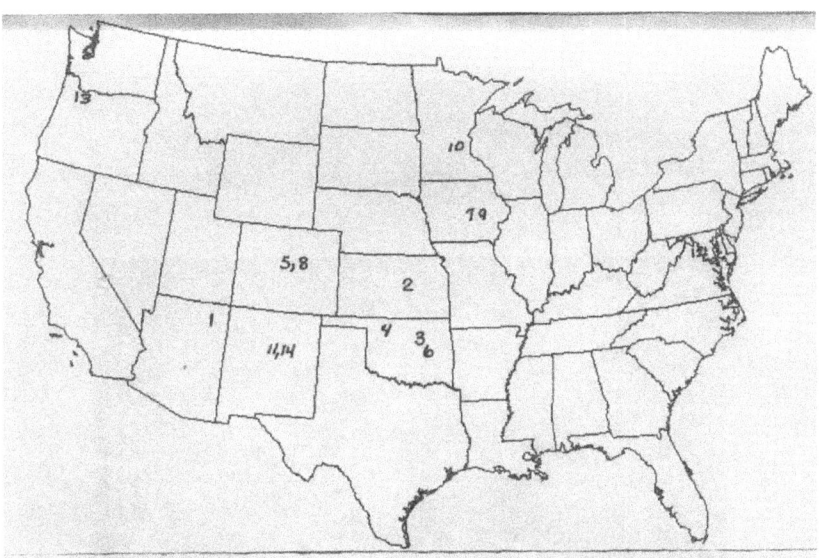

1. 1958 Graduated, Ganado Mission High School
2. 1958 College of Emporia; Emporia, Kansas
3. 1960 The University of Tulsa. Graduated June, 1962
4. 1962 August. Enid, OK. Child Welfare Worker. OK Welfare Department
5. 1963 University of Denver Graduate School of Social Work
6. 1964 June. Muskogee, OK. Child Welfare Worker, OK Welfare Department
7. 1965. June. Musquaki Indian Settlement; Tama, Iowa. Summer Volunteers, Presbyterian Church
8. 1965 September. 2nd year. Denver University School of Social Work. Graduated June 1966
9. 1966 June. University of Iowa Hospitals; Iowa City, IA. Medical Social Worker
10. 1967 June. Minneapolis, MN. Deputy Director, Upper Midwest American Indian Center; Minneapolis Public Schools Social Worker; Consultant, Minneapolis Health Department; Executive Director, Upper Midwest American Indian Center
11. 1973 Laguna – Albuquerque. BIA Supervisory Social Worker, Southern Pueblos Agency. 1978, Area Social Worker, BIA Albuquerque Area
12. 1989 Deputy Director & Acting Director, BIA Social Services Division, Washington, DC
13. 1990 Area Social Worker, Portland Area Office. Portland, OR
14. 1999 July. Retired. Returned to Albuquerque

Right Place, Right Time

Sources

Note

[1] *Kawaigame Dzeeni, A Topical Dictionary of the Laguna Language.* (Pueblo of Laguna, 2011).

Laguna–English & English–Laguna Dictionary. Draft Edition. Undated.

Chapter 1

[2] *Census of the Paguate Band of Pueblo Indians, located in New Mexico:* Taken by James K. Allen, Superintendent, June 30, 1904. XI.

[3] Ibid. p.II.

[4] Witmer, Linda F. *The Indian Industrial School. Carlisle, Pennsylvania. 1879-1918.* Carlisle, PA. Permission granted by the Cumberland County Historical Society. Carlisle, PA: The Indian Industrial School, Carlisle, Pennsylvania, 1879-1918.

[5] *Report of Sheep Dipped for Scabies, U. S. Department of Agriculture, Bureau of Animal Industry.* September 16, 1920.

[6] Marmon, Kathryn, "Native Mission. Laguna Scouts prominent in Apache Campaign", *New Mexican.* August, 2002. 58, 59.

[7] "Frank Hudson (American football)". http://en.wikipedia. Org/wiki/Frank_Hudson_(American_football).

[8] Parsons, Elsie Clews, "Laguna Genealogies", *Anthropological Papers of the American Museum of Natural History.* Vol. XIX, Part V. (New York: Published by order of the Trustees. 1923). 181.

Right Place, Right Time

Chapter 2

[9] Julyan, Robert. *The Place Names of New Mexico*, Revised Edition. (Albuquerque: University of New Mexico Press. 1988), 255.

[10] Information relayed to Robert C. Carr by Roland Johnson. September 9, 2013.

Chapter 4

[11] Edwards, John and Cate Edwards, and Jonathan Prince, Edited by. "Robert Carr", *Home. Blueprints of our Lives*. (New York: Harper Collins Publishers, 2006), 29.

Chapter 5

[12] Albuquerque Indian School. Retrieved from "https://wiki.familysearch.org/en/Albuquerque_Indian_School". Category: American Indian Schools.

[13] Jenkins, Sally. *The Real All Americans*. (New York, London, Toronto, Sydney, Auckland: Doubleday, 2007).

[14] Anderson, Lars. *Carlisle vs. Army*. (New York: Random House Trade Paperbacks, 2007).

Chapter 7

[15] Haldeman, E. M., Chief Engineer, Ganado Mission. "A Short Historical Sketch of Ganado Mission, Ganado, Arizona", *Historical Sketch of Ganado Mission, Ganado Arizona*, Owned and Operated by the Board of National Missions United Presbyterian Church, U.S.A. April, 1967.

[16] E-mail. Marilyn Watchman Dalton to Robert Carr, April 10, 2013.

[17] Ibid.

[18] Gridley, Marion E. "Roe B. Lewis (Pima-Papago) Educational Counselor", *Indians of Today*. Fourth Edition. (I.C.F.P; INC. 1971). 390.

[19] Edwards, John, 28-30.

Chapter 9

[20] Ibid. 30.

[21] E-mail. Linda Sadler Myers to Robert Carr, April 8, 2013.

Chapter 10

[22] Gridley, 390.

Chapter 12

[23] Letter from Director of Development and Alumni Giving, The University of Denver, to Robert Carr, March 25, 2013.

Chapter 13

[24] American Indian Centers Review Study, 1969 Minutes of American Indian Centers Committee. Community Health and Welfare Council of Hennepin County, Inc. Box 4, Folder 15. Social Welfare History Archives, Archives and Special Collections, University of Minnesota Libraries.

Chapter 14

[25] Morton, Secretary of the Interior, ET AL. v. Mancari ET AL Appeal from the United States District Court for the District of New Mexico. No. 73-362. Argued April 24, 1974 – Decided June 17, 1974.

www.ingramcontent.com/pod-product-compliance
Lightning Source LLC
Chambersburg PA
CBHW061254110426
42742CB00012BA/1910